CHRIST AT THE WALL IN THE CITY

FOREWORD BY DR. DOUG LOGAN, JR.

CHRIST AT THE WALL IN THE CITY

THE LIFE AND MINISTRY OF
DR. BILL KRISPIN

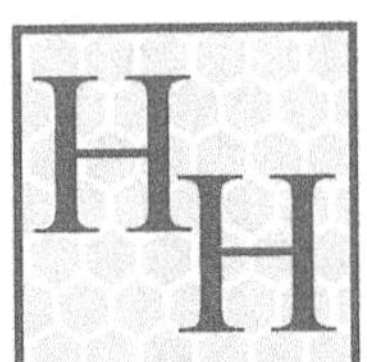

HONEYCOMB HOUSE PUBLISHING LLC
New Cumberland, Pennsylvania

Christ at the Wall in the City: The Life and Ministry of Bill Krispin

Published by Honeycomb House Publishing LLC
New Cumberland, Pennsylvania

Copyright ©2024 William Krispin
All rights reserved. Published 2024

ISBN (paperback): 978-0-9753934-4-4
ISBN (ebook): 978-0-9753934-5-1

Printed in the United States of America

CONTENTS

FOREWORD
A LIFE WOVEN INTO THE TAPESTRY OF PHILADELPHIA

But God has so composed the body, giving greater honor to the part that lacked it, that there may be no division in the body, but that the members may have the same care for one another. If one member suffers, all suffer together; if one member is honored, all rejoice together.

1 Corinthians 12:12–26 (ESV)

The Apostle Paul's profound illustration of the body of Christ speaks to the heart of Dr. William Krispin's life and ministry. Over five decades, Dr. Krispin has embodied the very essence of this Scripture, weaving his life into the vibrant and diverse tapestry of Philadelphia. His journey is a testament to the unity, diversity, and interdependence that Paul extols, a life spent in the service of the gospel, the local church, and the broader community. His vision was to establish churches serving as beacons of hope and reconciliation centers in every neighborhood.

Dr. Krispin's ministry began in Philadelphia as a pastor in the local church. This led to God calling him to plant a church in the core of South Philadephia in the mid-1960s. His pastoral care was not confined to the pulpit but extended into the very homes and hearts of the people he shepherded, as his pulpit would be a mobile one rolling out his love for the lost to the actual streets of the city. Bill's passion for people and reaching the unreached, he ventured into church planting, establishing new congregations that would become beacons of hope and a platform for a long-term ministry of training planters through various avenues. His vision was rooted in the belief that every neighborhood, no matter how overlooked, deserved a thriving local church where Christ's love could be tangibly experienced.

Dr. Krispin founded the Center for Urban Theological Studies by recognizing the critical need for theological education that speaks to urban ministry's unique challenges and opportunities. Here, he created a much-needed training space to make theological education accessible and affordable to urban leaders lacking contextualized training. At CUTS, he poured into the next generation of leaders, equipping them with the knowledge and passion needed to serve effectively in diverse and dynamic urban contexts. His teaching was not merely academic but a blend of rigorous scholarship and practical ministry insights drawn from his extensive experience. Students under his tutelage learned to navigate the complexities of urban life with a gospel-centered approach that addressed both spiritual and social needs. Bill was more than a professor and executive director to students from many different racial backgrounds; he was a Spiritual Father and mentor who journeyed with them from first year into a lifetime mentor and friend.

One of Dr. Krispin's most remarkable contributions has been his role as a unifier. He worked tirelessly to bridge divides in a city as diverse as Philadelphia, with its rich mosaic of cultures, races, and economic backgrounds. He fostered unity among pastors and churches across racial, denominational, and socioeconomic lines, believing that the body of Christ must reflect the unity for which Jesus prayed. Through initiatives, dialogues, and collaborative efforts, he helped build a network of relationships that transcended traditional barriers, modeling a biblical and transformative unity.

Over the years, Dr. Krispin became known as a pastor of pastors, a mentor, and a guide to many who themselves were leading congregations. Doc has a "personable pastoral-touch" that draws men in and helps them to be very vulnerable and personal. His wisdom, humility, and steadfast faith provided a fountain of support and encouragement. Doc is simply a relational dude who loves a lot of pastors. He loves to see them become better, more educated, more effective, and overall better men of God. Pastors found Dr. Krispin to be a sage in times of personal and ministry challenges. Doc often understood their struggles, and he just knew how to listen, love, and lead them through the many trials and challenges they faced in ministry and life. His investment in the lives of Pastors of various races and places has had a multiplying effect as they, in turn, shepherd their own flocks, indirectly placing his fingerprint on many church's gospel impact on the city.

From demography to prayer rides through the city, Dr. Krispin's approach to ministry has always been profoundly missiological and grounded in a profound understanding of the varying contexts of the city. As an urban missiologist, he trained many church planters and pastors on how to engage with the city's changing landscapes, identifying and responding to the evolving needs of its people. Incarnational Ministry is a staple of his ministry as he is involved in proclamation and presence, being a constant and committed part of the community he serves. His strategies for outreach and engagement have been marked by creativity, resilience, and an unwavering commitment to the gospel.

As you read through the pages of this book, you will journey through the life of a man whose ministry has been marked by faithfulness, innovation, and a deep love for God and people. Dr. Krispin's story is not just a chronicle of one man's achievements but a testament to what God can do through a willing and obedient man of God. His life reminds us that in the body of Christ, every part is indispensable, every role vital, and every person honored.

I'd be remiss if I did not mention that I am a grateful recipient of Doc's love and shepherding as a student of Bill and a spiritual son. Bill has had an indelible mark on my life, from helping to feed my family to assisting me in purchasing a car. My role as a seminary president and dean of the school of urban ministry was in many ways formed from the shaping and shepherding of Doc. I find myself lovingly saying his sayings and remembering conversations that molded my ministry and modeled for me what it looks like to lead pastors. I am now a spiritual father to several amazing spiritual sons.

Dr. Krispin's legacy in Philadelphia as a pastor, educator, pastor-of-pastors, and urban missiologist is one of transformation, unity, and enduring impact. Bill's story inspires us to see the city with new eyes, engage with our communities with renewed vigor, and trust that God can use each uniquely to build His kingdom. May this book be a beacon of hope and a call to faithful service for all who read it!

Doug Logan, Jr., PhD
President, Grimké Seminary and College
Author of *On the Block* and *The Soul Winning Church*

PREFACE
GREAT IS YOUR FAITHFULNESS

This hymn summarizes the great faithfulness of God to all who believe and has been especially true in my life.

> Great is Thy faithfulness, O God my Father;
> there is no shadow of turning with Thee;
> Thou changest not, Thy compassions they fail not;
> as Thou hast been, Thou forever wilt be.
>
> *Refrain:*
> Great is Thy faithfulness! Great is Thy faithfulness!
> Morning by morning new mercies I see;
> all I have needed Thy hand hath provided:
> great is Thy faithfulness, Lord, unto me!
>
> Summer and winter, and springtime and harvest;
> sun, moon, and stars in their courses above
> join with all nature in manifold witness
> to Thy great faithfulness, mercy, and love.
>
> *Refrain*
>
> Pardon for sin and a peace that endureth,
> Thine own dear presence to cheer and to guide;
> strength for today and bright hope for tomorrow:
> blessings all mine with ten thousand beside!
>
> Great is Thy faithfulness! Great is Thy faithfulness!
> Morning by morning new mercies I see;
> All I have needed Thy hand hath provided;
> Great is Thy faithfulness! Great is Thy faithfulness!
> Great is Thy faithfulness, Lord, unto me![1]

---

1 Thomas O. Chisholm, "Great Is Thy Faithfulness" (hymn), 1923, public domain.

INTRODUCTION
BARNABAS, SON OF ENCOURAGEMENT

Over the years God has used the life and ministry of Barnabas, the Son of Encouragement, to motivate and direct me as I seek to minister to others. The following is what I've learned from him.

RAISING UP LEADERS FOR THE HARVEST

Leaders are greatly needed for the God-given mission of the church. Jesus gave this charge to his disciples on the occasion of his ascension into heaven: "Go therefore and make disciples of all nations, baptizing them in the name of the Father and of the Son and of the Holy Spirit, teaching them to observe all that I have commanded you; and lo, I am with you always, even to the end of the age" (Matt. 28:19–20, ESV). And Acts 1:8: "But you will receive power when the Holy Spirit comes on you; and you will be my witnesses in Jerusalem, and in all Judea and Samaria, and to the ends of the earth."

"Go into the whole world to make disciples of all nations"—really, *all nations?* That seems overwhelming and yet that was the mission. All disciples of Christ were to do this. Remarkably, by the end of the lives of the apostles, this mission had been accomplished.

How is this possible? This seems impossible for a group of twelve to do. And yet it happened because they saw their mission to be to make disciples of those who believe everywhere. Rarely does the church today see this as its mission. The central command in Matthew 28:19–20 is to "make disciples." To accomplish this, they were to be going ever outward with the gospel "even to the ends of the earth." As they were going, they were to baptize all believers and then to "teach them to obey all that Christ had commanded"—all that Christ commanded.

This is discipleship, but it is also the core principle of mentoring.

13

We know from the Book of Acts that the early church wrestled with this command. It was not immediately clear to them that God meant all peoples everywhere, including the Gentiles. How else could you understand this? Upon reflection, they could have thought that Christ meant the Jews of the dispersion. After all, that was who was gathered in Jerusalem for the feast of Pentecost (Acts 2:5–12). We see Peter wrestling with this in Acts 9:32–11:18.

Next, we see Barnabas being commissioned by the apostles in Jerusalem to go to Antioch to check out what is going on there, where Gentiles were coming to faith in Christ (Acts 11:11–20). "When he arrived and saw the evidence of the grace of God, he was glad and encouraged them all to remain true to the Lord with all their hearts. He was a good man, full of the Holy Spirit and faith, and a great number of people were brought to the Lord" (Acts 11:23–24). Barnabas had the spiritual discernment to see how God was working among the Gentiles, and he was led to affirm them as genuine believers and to work on their behalf to provide leadership to them, so that they could grow in grace and in a knowledge of the Lord. As a result of the great door of ministry that opened in Antioch, he is led by the Spirit to go to the city of Tarsus in Turkey to find Saul and bring him to Antioch to work alongside him in discipling the many new believers there. They continued to labor there for a full year. (See Acts 11:25–26.) Barnabas and Paul became partners in the harvest, with Barnabas as the leader. From here we can follow Barnabas as he mentors Paul to be an apostle to the Gentiles. Barnabas knew that this was God's call on Paul's life, as he was the one who brought Paul and introduced him to the apostles and the church in Jerusalem. At his conversion on the road to Damascus, God had told Paul, then Saul of Tarsus, through Ananias, that he would be His apostle to the Gentiles (Acts 9:15–16).

In Acts 11:9–18, Peter reports back to the church in Jerusalem on what has occurred among the Gentiles. In Acts 15, Barnabas and Paul report to the apostles in Jerusalem on the fruit of their first missionary journey. During that journey, their steps had been dogged by the Judaizers, who insisted that any Gentiles who believed must be circumcised. After debate, the apostles determined that Gentiles were indeed authentic believers and did not need to be circumcised. And so, the debate over the meaning of the great commission was finally settled. Jesus indeed sends his followers to seek to reach all the peoples of the world.

CHALLENGES TO THE MISSION OF THE CHURCH TODAY

The church is still wrestling with the call of the great commission today. We tend to write off different people groups because of lifestyle, ethnicity, alienation, and so on. In so doing, we consciously fail to bring the gospel to them.

We live in a world with a rapidly changing culture that is often uncomfortable to the church. The church is panting to keep up. The reality is that we are moving in the direction of irrelevancy. Cultural change is moving faster and faster. We tend to make changes ten years after a change has come. Occasionally, we might adjust to face change as it happens now, but almost never do we anticipate change that is coming and work to address it in our life and message.

The training of church leaders has too often been relegated to seminaries that focus on interpreting the Scripture in its original context rather than how to apply Scripture to our world today. One learns relatively little about contemporary life and culture. The result is that seminaries do little to train people to be leaders of the church in contemporary culture. We need leaders who see where the culture is moving and step up to lead the church to address that culture.

Such training, I believe, will not come from seminaries but will come out of churches that are intentionally raising up leaders through mentoring, which is a lost dynamic in the church today. Mentoring is needed to raise up leaders for expanding the ministry of the church into new and strategic areas.

We must also mentor leaders from the younger generation to rise to fill the shoes of those who have preceded them. Too many pastors continue to serve as the lead person in congregations to the very end of their lives. In far too many cases, when the leader dies, the church dies with him, because there is no one in the church to take his place.

It is a common phenomenon today that new church plants are led by a younger leader who reaches people in their own generation, who then grow old together. The day of the multi-generational church is over. Church youth today will rarely attend the church of their youth when they enter adulthood. If today's church does not reach the next young generations with the gospel, these churches, too, will die.

We are facing a real crisis in the church. From an informal survey that I do when speaking to a church on the mission of the church, I have learned that ninety-five percent of those who attend church regularly come to faith and commit to a church between the ages of eighteen and twenty-five. But it is also true that many of those who grow up in a church will leave the church altogether during those same years. Remarkably, many committed Christian youth emerge into leaders through evangelism and discipleship in campus fellowships during their college years; yet, sadly, they return home after college to churches that do not invest in their continued development and nor place them into leadership roles alongside older, mature leaders.

I can tell you that my most effective years in ministry have been the years following my "retirement." I have had the opportunity to invest in the lives of many young leaders, mentoring and advising them in their ministries.

Key Principles Foundational to Mentoring

1. The John the Baptist principle: "He must increase, but I must decrease" (John 3:30). John the Baptist understood that his role was to be the forerunner of Christ, preparing the people for the coming of the Savior.

2. Second Timothy 2:2: "And the things you have heard me say in the presence of many witnesses entrust to reliable people who will also be qualified to teach others." Pass on what you have been taught to faithful believers so that they too can teach others.

3. We are privileged to allow the younger generation to stand on our shoulders to see and go further than we have.

LESSONS ON MENTORING FROM BARNABAS AND PAUL

Here we will address what mentoring is and examine the ministry of Barnabas investing in the development of the Apostle Paul and others.

Barnabas is one the most important people in the New Testament, yet he is rarely mentioned in the church today. Once you get to know him, you will understand why he goes unnoticed. It is because he was often a quiet, behind-the-scenes kind of guy. Rarely was he the high profile, up-front guy. But his influence was great…as he chose to work through others.

Barnabas is first mentioned in Acts 4:36–37. There we read: "Joseph, a Levite from Cyprus, whom the apostles called Barnabas (which means Son of Encouragement), sold a field he owned and brought the money and put it at the apostles' feet." Note the following:

1. His name was really Joseph, a Levite from the Island of Cyprus in the Mediterranean.

2. His name was changed by the apostles to "Barnabas" because he was a "Son of Encouragement." Wow! So great was his ministry of encouragement that

that became his name. We will see how encouragement was his spiritual gift. In this passage, we first see this ministry in his generosity in giving to meet the personal, physical, and financial needs of believers in the church. This is a key principle of mentoring—encouragement, saying to others that "yes, you can."

3. Barnabas is next mentioned in Acts 9:26–30, in connection with the conversion of Saul of Tarsus. How anxious would you have been to meet Saul? After all, he was the leader of those who had killed Stephen in Acts 7:54–8:1. And when he was converted to be a believer in Christ, he was on the road to the city of Damascus to persecute believers there. As a new believer he desired to give testimony of his new faith in Christ before the church in Jerusalem, but they were not anxious to meet him, fearing that it was a trick to capture and persecute them, too. It was Barnabas who overcame this fear; he was led to find Saul to hear his testimony. Believing that he was a genuine believer, Barnabas brings Saul to the apostles and himself bears witness before the church of the genuineness of Saul's conversion. What encouragement! How many of us had a Barnabas early in our walk with the Lord who took the time to get to know us and who came to believe that God was truly working in us—even though our stories before we knew Christ were stories of great brokenness and sin? Barnabas really believed 2 Corinthians 5:17: "Therefore, if anyone is in Christ, he is a new creation; the old has gone, the new has come!"

4. And so begins the long partnership of Barnabas with Saul (whose name is later changed to Paul). They are eventually commissioned by the Antioch Church to be missionaries together to the Gentiles (Acts 13:1–12). During that first missionary journey, Barnabas and Paul minister together as one. As you read the account of their ministry, you can't tell who does what. Initially, it is "Barnabas and Paul"; later it's "Paul and Barnabas." Barnabas is a spiritual giant who is quite content to let Paul shine. Here we see Paul standing on the shoulders of Barnabas in the work of the ministry. In a very real sense, Paul is the spiritual son of Barnabas. Their ministry together continues through Acts 15, when they go together to Jerusalem to defend the gospel coming to the Gentiles without the requirement of circumcision.

5. But our story would not be complete without talking about the division that came between Barnabas and Paul. On that first missionary

journey, they had also taken John Mark along with them. John Mark was a nephew of Barnabas, and he is also the one who wrote the Gospel of Mark. At that time, Mark was immature, and he grew weary in the work of ministry to the point that he gave up and headed back home. As Paul and Barnabas prepare for a second missionary journey, Barnabas once again wants to take John Mark along. Paul balks at this. This leads to a parting of the ways between them. Paul heads one direction with Silas, and Barnabas takes John Mark and goes again to Cyprus, his home country. But this is not the end of the story. It is Barnabas who continues to disciple John Mark for gospel ministry. And Paul and John Mark later reconcile and team up again. But it was Barnabas who had prepared John Mark for this, having mentored him to become a leader in the mission of the church. Note the following passages:

Colossians 4:10: My fellow prisoner Aristarchus sends you his greetings, as does Mark, the cousin of Barnabas. (You have received instructions about him; if he comes to you, welcome him.)

Philemon 23–24: Epaphras, my fellow prisoner in Christ Jesus, sends you greetings. And so do Mark, Aristarchus, Demas and Luke, my fellow workers.

Second Timothy 4:11: Only Luke is with me. Get Mark and bring him with you because he is helpful to me in my ministry.

Barnabas' Ministry Is in Keeping with Second Timothy 2:2

Let us summarize what all this means for the preparation of leaders in the church. Of particular importance is the role of leadership to mentor, or disciple, believers for the work of ministry for the building up of the body of Christ is of great importance. (See Ephesians 4:11–16.) The Barnabas story is a beautiful picture of 2 Timothy 2:2: "And the things you have heard me say in the presence of many witnesses entrust to reliable men who will also be qualified to teach others."

Barnabas	Paul	Silas	
	John Mark	Timothy	to others also
		Titus	

So, who is your Barnabas? And who are you Barnabas to? The gospel that has changed our lives is a treasure not to sit on but to be passed on to others. God calls each one of us to the ministry of Barnabas. Yes, the ministry of encouragement is essential if the body of Christ is to be fully discipled and mobilized in God's great mission of reaching the lost.

Stop now and give thanks to God for those who have extended Barnabas encouragement ministry to you. But also pray that God would use you as a Barnabas to someone else. Pass on what you have received so that the light of Christ may shine in and through others, to the glory and praise of our great God and Savior, Jesus Christ!

ENCOURAGEMENT IN THE BIBLE: NEW TESTAMENT ONE-ANOTHERING PASSAGES

A number of passages in the New Testament outline how we are to minister to one another and carry out Barnabas ministry. These passages give a clear description of how Christians are to actively communicate the gospel in daily life, one to another. This includes such passages as:

Ephesians 1:3–6	God himself "one-anothers" those who are his
Hebrews 3:13 and 10:24–25	Encourage one another.
Romans 14:19 and 1 Thessalonians 5:11	Edify one another.
Ephesians 4:31–32	Be kind one to another.
1 Peter 5:5 and Ephesians 5:20–21	Submit to one another.
John 13:34–35, 15:12–13; Romans 13:18; 1 Peter 1:22	Love one another.
1 Peter 4:7–10; Romans 12:10a, 13; 1 Timothy 3:2; Titus 1:8; Hebrews 13:1–2	Show hospitality one to another.
Colossians 3:13	Forgive one another.
1 Thessalonians 4:13–18	Comfort one another.
James 5:16 and Romans 15:30	Pray for one another.

Galatians 6:2	Bear one another's burdens.
1 Peter 5:14 and 2 Corinthians 13:11	Greet one another.
Hebrews 10:24	Consider one another.
Romans 15:7	Accept one another.
Ephesians 4:1–3	Forbear with one another.
1 Corinthians 12:21–26	Care for one another.
1 Peter 4:10	Minister to one another.
Romans 12:16	Live in harmony.
Romans 12:10	Prefer one another.
James 5:16a	Confess your faults one to another.
Ephesians 4:25	We are members one of another.
Colossians 3:8–9	Don't lie to one another.
Galatians 5:15	Don't consume one another.
James 4:11	Don't speak evil of one another.

ENCOURAGEMENT IN THE BIBLE:
THE FRUIT OF THE SPIRIT—NEW LIFE IN CHRIST

Of equal importance are the fruit of the Spirit found in Galatians 5:13ff. Here Paul contrasts life in the flesh with life in the Spirit. It is the fruit of the Spirit that we are to cultivate in our daily lives and that prepares us for our Barnabas one-anothering ministry.

> You, my brothers and sisters, were called to be free. But do not use your freedom to indulge the flesh; rather, serve one another humbly in love. For the entire law is fulfilled in keeping this one command: "Love your neighbor as yourself." If you bite and devour each other, watch out or you will be destroyed by each other.

> So I say, walk by the Spirit, and you will not gratify the desires of the flesh. For the flesh desires what is contrary to the Spirit, and the Spirit what is contrary to the flesh. They are in conflict with each other, so that

you are not to do whatever you want. But if you are led by the Spirit, you are not under the law.

The acts of the flesh are obvious: sexual immorality, impurity, and debauchery; idolatry and witchcraft; hatred, discord, jealousy, fits of rage, selfish ambition, dissensions, factions and envy; drunkenness, orgies, and the like. I warn you, as I did before, that those who live like this will not inherit the kingdom of God.

But the fruit of the Spirit is love, joy, peace, forbearance, kindness, goodness, faithfulness, gentleness and self-control. Against such things there is no law. Those who belong to Christ Jesus have crucified the flesh with its passions and desires. Since we live by the Spirit, let us keep in step with the Spirit. Let us not become conceited, provoking and envying each other. (Galatians 5:13–26)

I encourage you to cultivate these graces in your life. To do this is to go from self-centeredness to living for others out of the rich mercy and grace of God. I recommend that you consider all these spiritual characteristics to develop a growth plan. It is always helpful to do this in a small group where spiritual accountability can take place.

1

CHILDHOOD IN CHICAGO

I was born in 1943 into the family of the six children of Victor and Gladys Krispin. Our family was a strong Christian family in which it was a daily practice to have family devotions led by my father, who would pray for each of his children by name. We attended church regularly, often even for evening service at a wide variety of churches. I was exposed to the preaching of many of the day's great preachers.

A significant part of my early years was attending the original club of the Awana Youth Association with my brothers at the North Side Gospel Center where Lance B. Latham was pastor. The Awana system required the memorization of Scripture, and I memorized long passages of Scripture there. Later, during my college years, the Lord would use these memorized verses to bring me to conviction of my sin and my need of a Savior. We also attended the church's camp, Camp Awana in Wisconsin, where for two weeks we would work daily at the memorization of Scripture.

After my conversion at age nineteen while attending Northern Illinois State University, I returned to Chicago to attend North Park College, where I served weekly as a leader in Awana clubs of the North Side Gospel Center. These clubs used some ingenuous ways of discipling leaders. There was a job for everyone—from team leaders, to assistant team leaders, to devotional leaders, to manning the supply room where the game equipment was stored.

It was here that I formed a lifetime friendship with Arnie Mayer, who now lives in Seattle, Washington. Arnie served for about twenty years in Kenya developing a ministry called Cinema Leo, which took films around to many villages to share the Gospel. The ministry continues to this day under entirely indigenous leadership. Following his service in Kenya, Arnie returned to John Brown University in Siloam Springs, Arkansas to serve as a professor of film and broadcast media.

CHILDHOOD TRAUMA

When I was twelve or thirteen years old, we faced a major trauma in our life as a family. The 1950s was a decade of radical urban transformation as a huge demographic shift was taking place. During the years Eisenhower was president, the interstate highway system was built throughout America—55,000 miles in all. Five different interstate highway spurs were put in Chicago, cutting large swaths throughout the city; 350,000 families were displaced. Ours was one of those families. Because all of this happened at one time, the housing stock of Chicago greatly shrunk. People were forced out of the city—mass migration to the suburbs began. Our family was one of those families. Because so many families were displaced at the same time, there was no place for us to go. for many, many families—including ours. Month after month, my mother would go out daily looking for an apartment. But nobody wanted, or needed, to rent to a large family. So we continued to live in a large apartment until everybody else had moved out. With one month to go before demolition of our building, we were forced to move across the street into another building scheduled to be demolished a year later. The search for a permanent home continued. Finally, after a long search, one was found. But we quickly learned that the realtor we were working with had lied. He had told the landlord that there were three children, while there were five of us at that time. The landlord immediately raised the rent $25 per month, which at the time was no small amount. As a result, my mother never felt at home there, even though the family lived there twenty years.

Now to the trauma. Prior to finding that home, we lived as squatters—the only family living in one and then another large, high-rise apartment building. During those two homeless years, there were nightly fires in the neighborhood. Kids would ignite them and then gather around to watch them burn. The fire department would not extinguish the fires but let them burn, working only to keep them from spreading. Most of these fires were at night. I would often lay awake all night because of fear of there being a fire in our building.

During those many months, I regularly had a crazy dream about a bear that would come and put me under the coffee table in the living room. I had no idea what triggered that crazy dream. This dream endured until I was fifty-four years old—yes, fifty-four years old. After almost forty years of having that dream regularly, I came home from an evening of teaching and sat down on the sofa to watch the program on TV that my wife Mary was watching. The program was about family homelessness in New York City. The moderator was interviewing an eleven-year-old girl. He asked her, "What is that you most fear?" She replied, "It's the sirens in the night." I immediately said, "That's it." That is what triggered the dream—it was the sirens in the night. After that, I never had the dream again.

As a child, I shared a bedroom with my twin brothers. I decided to call them up to ask them simply, "Do you remember the sirens in the night?" Both immediately broke down and cried. I also called my oldest brother with the same question, and he, too, cried. They all said that they had lain awake all night long in fear. I then asked all of them, "Why did we never talk together about it?" We were just stuffing it inside and carrying it into our adult years.

During this entire period, our family continued to attend church faithfully. Nobody ever asked us how we were doing. We would ask for prayers. And there were members who had rentals in buildings they owned. Nothing. This began a process in my heart of shutting out God. This lasted until I was nineteen.

Because of the white flight happening rapidly in Chicago due to the displacement of households in the path of an expressway, our church rapidly transitioned from being an urban church to being a commuter church. Slowly, people moved to other churches closer to their homes. Church after church in our area closed their doors. From my perspective then, as churches left, I thought that God was leaving, too. I did not yet see how God was raising up new congregations in their place. It was another decade before I learned to look at things differently.

Though I was not yet a true believer, God used this experience later to open my heart to giving my life over to live and minister in the city. It was also the beginning of the development of a holistic concept of ministry.

2

College, Seminary, and First Steps in Ministry

As I said, scripture memorization was a major part of my upbringing. The key passage I memorized early on was Ephesians 2:8–10. God used this passage to bring me to faith in Christ when I was just nineteen years old.

Coming to Faith in Christ

I was a student at Northern Illinois University, and I was very ambivalent to Christianity. I simply did not believe it. I was in the class of a history professor who was a blatant atheist and whose mission it was to destroy the faith of anyone who believed. In a course on Western history encompassing the Reformation, we were given an assignment to go to the library to the reserve section of books for our course and read some passages in a book relevant to one's religious background. True to form for me, I waited until the last minute to do the assignment.

When I got to the library, there was only one book on the shelf relevant to my side of the Reformation—a book of sermons by Martin Luther. It was a big book. I decided to open the book at random and read whatever section it brought up. It turned out to be a sermon on Ephesians 2:8–10. As I read it, I became convicted of the sin in my life. I was particularly struck by the phrase: "and that not of yourself; it is the gift of God, not of works lest anyone should boast." That night I confessed faith in Christ and began my walk as a Christian.

Over the course of my life, God used this passage on many occasions to remind me that who I was as a Christian and any good that I did was not of my own doing but rather was the work of a gracious God. This has been particularly evident in the periods of major illness I experienced throughout the course of my life, when God put me in bed to remind me to rely on him and not on myself. I will say more on this later.

From College to Seminary

In 1962, I decided to transfer to North Park College in Chicago to continue my college education. There I majored in History and Philosophy. My college years are a total blur because I was a commuter student at a residential college, and I worked full–time throughout college. I was on campus only for classes and rehearsal for the Chapel Choir, in which I sang tenor. We were blessed to have a gifted director who was also an expert organist. Though I never again sang in a choir, I did, from time to time, sing solos.

As I neared the time of my graduation, the Vietnam War buildup was beginning, and I was almost certain to be drafted after college if I didn't take steps to continue my educational deferment. I was weary of schooling, and I wasn't eager to further my education, but I certainly did not want to go to Vietnam. Consequently, I decided to go to seminary.

I considered several seminaries, but finally decided on Westminster Seminary, in the Philadelphia area—at the recommendation of my father, who told me that he thought college had messed me up and that I needed to get my head straightened out. So I started studies at Westminster in 1966. At Westminster, I was taught from a single theological perspective. I soon discovered my father was right!

I found seminary to be challenging in several ways. First, living at the seminary put me in a bubble where all that was talked about were theological arguments. Secondly, the location of seminary—in the suburbs of metro Philadelphia—was not convenient to any public transportation that would enable me to get to the city easily. So I found the isolation stifling.

When I entered my second year of seminary, I was able to obtain an internship at Tenth Presbyterian Church in Center City Philadelphia, under the Reverend Dr. Mariano DiGangi. Initially, my role was to serve as the pastor to the teenagers of the church and to participate in leading the morning worship service. It was a privilege to meet every Saturday morning with Dr. DiGangi to discuss my calling to the ministry and our work of ministry at the church.

Hannah McFetridge

When Dr. DiGangi realized that my calling was to work in an urban setting, he assigned me to go to South Philadelphia to assist in the youth ministry at Evangel Presbyterian Church. The youth ministry was under the leadership of Mrs. Hannah McFetridge. Prior to my arrival, Miss Hannah, as the kids called her, carried out youth ministry to almost 200 children and teenagers without any assistance. At seventy-five years old, she had the energy of a teenager.

She had remarkable control over all that happened at the youth meeting. She was even known to referee a basketball game in the gym in her high heel shoes. She had no clue about all the rules, but she had two rules that she particularly sought to enforce. They were "You may not hit" and "You may not trip." She would assess an appropriate number of penalty shots based on the severity of the offense. She was known to give *ten* penalty shots for grievous actions.

Each night Miss Hannah would give a thirty-minute talk on passages of the Bible to the young people. She loved those kids dearly, and it was evident in all that she did. These were street kids. Few had a tie to any churches. She pledged to the children that she would raise the funds for them to go to college if they would finish high school and decided to go on to further education. Eight young people in that group ultimately became pastors of churches in Philadelphia, and she assisted them financially with both college and seminary. She was not a wealthy person, but she had a wealth of friends who joined her in supporting this effort.

Evangel Church had only six members, all over the age of seventy. At the end of the year, Miss Hannah told me that if I started a new church in South Philadelphia, she could let her church close. And this is what ultimately happened. In 1968, Mary and I moved to South Philadelphia to begin a new ministry.

JACK MILLER

I met Dr. Jack Miller in the very first class I took at the seminary—a course on apologetics, taught by Dr. Cornelius Van Til. We formed an enduring relationship. He had a significant role in my receiving a call to be a church planter of the Orthodox Presbyterian Church in South Philadelphia.

At the end of my third year in seminary, Jack arranged a lunch with the Reverend Roy Oliver, who was the General Secretary of the Committee on Home Missions of the Orthodox Presbyterian Church. As a result of that meeting, the Home Mission Committee determined to call me to be a church planter in South Philadelphia.

And so, Mary and I moved to South Philadelphia in June 1968. This occurred while I was still in seminary, with two years yet ahead of me. It's important to note that while I did not get ordained until the spring of 1970, I was still doing the work of a church planter.

What I've Learned

Perhaps the most important thing I learned when I started writing these memoirs was the significance of my first three years of ministry. These years changed the direction of my life. Let me review:

1. In early 1968, through the influence of Dr. Jack Miller, I was called to plant a church in Philadelphia, under the sponsorship of the Orthodox Presbyterian Church.

2. At the time, I was in my third year of four at Westminster. So, I began my ministry while still a seminary student. This was highly unusual.

3. We moved to South Philadelphia in June 1968. For one year we lived in rented quarters.

4. I graduated from Westminster in May 1969.

5. In the spring of 1969 we purchased a storefront at 1162 S. 15th Street.

6. That same year, shortly after purchasing the storefront property, I answered a knock at my door and met a 6'8" man who filled the doorway. He didn't say hello or tell me his name; he simply said, "Why are you here?" I told him I was here to start a church. He said, "Are you going to do this like all the other white folks who ignore what God is already doing in the Black church?" I said that I hadn't thought about that.

I expected he was going to tell me to go back to where I came from. Instead, he smiled and said, "Come with me and I will show you what God is doing through the Black church." He meant that. He began to take me everywhere he went. One of the places we went to was a prayer group of bi-vocational pastors which met at the Manna Bible Institute at 6 a.m. on Thursday. There they prayed for their churches and for the city.

We had been discussing the need for an urban Christian school. Then, on August 15, 1969, as we prayed, one brother interrupted us to say that God's way was to work through his people. That group then decided to open a Christian school *three weeks later* on September 8th. But we had no students, no teachers, no facilities, no books or desks for students and teachers. I thought it was impossible.

Because I was the only full-time person in the group, I became the feet for project. Amazingly, the school did open on September

15th with fifty-five students and four teachers in a rent-free building, with all the books and eauipment. The prayer group became the board of the school and I was asked to serve as the treasurer/financial director.

7. Just two years later, in 1971, that same board began discussing their own need for ministry and theological training. This led to the birth of what became the Center for Urban Theological Studies (CUTS).

All this happened in just my first four years in ministry. What young leader is given such an opportunity for ministry? I was just 26 years old when the Christian school opened.

From this new beginning, the Lord redirected me to serve the larger body of Christ in Philadelphia. I became an advocate for the unity and diversity of Christ's church in Philadelphia.

This led me to consider how my view had changed from those formative years. They changed in several ways:

1. My view of the church changed. I now saw a racially, ethnically, and theologically diverse church. But in my study of scripture, particularly First Corinthians 12:12–26, I came to understand that we were one church, with many parts, and members together.

2. I learned that I could work with this diversity using the Learning Together with an Open Bible concept developed early on by CUTS.

3. Often I was only reformed and presbyterian person in the classroom. Most were Pentecostals and Baptists. Using the Learning Together with an open bible concept I came to appreciate different theological perspectives. One of these were the spiritual gifts of I Corinthians 12 and Romans 12. I have become persuaded that the spiritual gifts continue to the present day. While I am not a practicing charismatic, I do accept the gifts as for the present day.

4. Further, almost half of CUTS students were women, serving in various leadership roles, including preachers, teachers, and pastors. I became comfortable with women serving in these roles.

3

MINISTRY IN SOUTH PHILADELPHIA

In the summer of 1969, our ministry in South Philadelphia began with having a Vacation Bible School, which was well-attended by neighborhood youth. We were able to use Mount Hebron Baptist Church on Wharton Street for this ministry. In the fall that followed, we began a youth club for middle and high schoolers, also using Mount Hebron.

In June 1969 we purchased 1162 South 15th Street as our home and ministry base. This was a unique property because it was two row-house units connected back-to-back and going from 15th Street through to Hicks Street behind the buildings. The front building was a storefront and a four-bedroom house. The back building had a large garage room which served as our youth center. My office and a small meeting room were on the second floor. We remained in that house until 1980 when we moved to Germantown.

WHAT GOD WAS ALREADY DOING

Even before we began formal ministry at our home, I received a knock at my door that would change the trajectory of our work.

I was working on the house to get it ready for ministry when I heard a knock at the door. When I opened the door, I found a 6'8" man standing there. He didn't introduce himself. He just said, "What are you doing here?"

I didn't know what to say. Finally, I said that I was here to start a new church. He then said, "Are you going to do this like all the other white folks who pretend that God is not carrying on his work through the Black church?"

I remember stammering, "Until you asked, I guess that's what I was doing."

I thought he would say, "Pack your bags and go back to where you came from." Instead, he smiled and said, "If you want, come with me, and I'll introduce you to the Black church of Philadelphia." And that is what he did.

Since we had not yet begun the ministry, I was free to go with him. It turned out that he lived two blocks south of our home. One of the first places he took me was a 6am Thursday morning prayer meeting of bi-vocational pastors at the Manna Bible Institute, which was then located on 40th Street in the Mantua section of the city. I found ten to twelve pastors gathered there to pray for their ministries and for the city before they went to work for the day. These men took me under their wings as a fledgling minister and would have a significant impact on the direction of my ministry.

PACS—The Christian School

I first attended the Thursday morning prayer meeting in July of 1969. The scene on the streets of our neighborhoods at that time was a desperate one for children. Gang street violence was on the rise. Over 150 teens were killed each year from 1969 to 1973. The first three funerals I conducted were for teens killed in gang violence.

The prayer group began to discuss options for the youth. They prayed weekly that somehow God would raise up a Christian school that would be safe place for learning. Every week, we prayed the same prayer. Finally, on August 15th, 1969, in the middle of praying, one brother stopped us and said: "We keep praying that God would do something. I think that God's way is to work through his people. God has put this on our hearts, and I think that He means for us to do something about it."

And so, before we finished the prayer meeting that day, the decision was made to open a Christian school—on September 8, 1969! I thought this was pure folly. We had no students, no teachers, no furnishings, no books, and no place to meet. How was this to happen in just three weeks?

Since I was the only full-time pastor in the group and was just starting a new church, I was asked to be the feet for this project. The group met regularly to plan and pray, and slowly, over the three weeks, the pieces started to come together. We found a rent-free facility in a run-down church at Ninth and Lehigh Streets. The building needed everything. We found five teachers willing to work for a low salary. But we still had none of the other pieces necessary to run a school.

The day before we were to open, still having no furnishings and no books, we heard the doorbell ring. Opening the door, I found a man who said he had a truckload of school furnishings and instructional materials. What was found in that truckload was the exact number of furnishings for the number of students we were expecting the next day, plus all the textbooks we needed for kindergarten through sixth grade. These supplies had come from a Catholic school that had closed and learned of our school from the Friend's community desk at 15th and Cherry Streets. God had put me into this project to show me that when he builds the house, the one who labors doesn't do so in vain. This was one of my first faith lessons.

So, by God's grace, we opened a Christian school on September 8th. This was one of the earliest Christian schools in the city. The first one serving the urban community was Timothy Christian Academy, serving the Hispanic community and located on Reese Street, north of Lehigh, down Lehigh from where our school would be. The prayer group named our new school Central Christian School, which later became the Philadelphia Association for Christian Schools in Philadelphia (PACS). The Thursday prayer group became the board of the new school. Lasting relationships were formed.

Schools were started in two other locations within the first four years. However, this expansion from the original school happened too quickly. We weren't able to raise the funds necessary to support three schools. PACS continued with the original school in North Philadelphia. The Southwest School waa spun off as separate schools. Nevertheless, this forged the beginning of a very significant movement of Christian schools in Philadelphia.

EMMANUEL CHAPEL

We began holding worship services as Emmanuel Chapel in the storefront of our home in 1970. While our ministry started with children and youth, eventually adults from the community came as well. In addition, several young seminary students and their spouses also got involved. One of the students, Pastor Wilson Cummings, decided to move to South Philadelphia to join the team. He became the pastor when I stepped down in 1975 to give my full attention to the development of the Center for Urban Theological Studies (CUTS). He remains in South Philadelphia to this day.

By 1975, we had outgrown our storefront. We began to look for another place to meet for worship. We met for a period of time at the Clef Club of Philadelphia. This place left a lot to be desired. It didn't have central heat, so during the winter months we used a large, kerosene space heater to warm the place. We continued to look for a permanent location. Eventually, we were able to purchase a storefront on Broad Street at Elsworth Street. An anonymous donor gave the money for the purchase of the building. I suspect that this same person had previously given the funds to purchase a new Ford van.

Peace in the Night

Working with youth left us facing many challenges. Our neighborhood found itself between two opposing gangs who both were seeking to recruit the teens in our area into their gang. We made efforts to get parents to have their teens home and indoors by 7 p.m.

One night in August 1971, in the middle of the night, the large store windows were smashed out by someone. I've always assumed that it was one of the gangs, but I don't know for sure. Mary and I were sleeping in the bedroom just above the windows. But amazingly, our family slept through the whole incident.

When I awoke at 6 a.m., I went downstairs to get coffee only to find a police officer sitting in my living room. He told me that he had come into the house during the night and had yelled loudly to see if anyone was home. Believing that no one was home, he decided to stay for the night to guard the house.

When I realized what had happened, I had an amazing sense of peace. Shortly thereafter, a few local mothers came to give me the funds to replace the windows. They pleaded with me to not leave the neighborhood. All this was around 6 a.m. Not long after that, the phone rang again. It was my brother from Chicago, who called to tell me that the doctors had found inoperable cancer in my mother. Still, the peace remained.

At around 7 a.m., the phone rang. It was a pastor friend, Pastor Henry Corey, who was ministering in California. He said he was calling to tell me that he and his wife had just prayed for us. It was just 4 a.m. in California. I thought to myself, "Ah, this is how God brought the peace."

Madeline Houston

One of the special friendships that developed at that time was with Madeline Houston. She was an amazing woman of God. Her testimony was that she was the Samaritan woman at the well. I'll leave it to your imagination to figure that one out.

She made killer fried chicken and sweet potato pie, and had a home business preparing meals for men in the local bars. When she delivered the meals to the bars, the men would take off their hats and wait until Madeline had "set the table"—with plasticware and napkins. No one ate until Madeline had asked the Lord's blessing on the food. She always managed to get in a short gospel message for them to ponder.

Madeline was known to carry a bag of Bibles with her wherever she went. She would stop people on the street to witness to them. People would frequently duck into doorways to avoid encountering her. She also went to local hospitals and would go from room to room, offering a prayer or handing out Bibles.

More than once, Madeline would call me in the middle of the night and say, "I just called to pray for you." Then she would read a brief passage of Scripture, pray, and say, "I'll talk with you later, darling." She never woke me up when she called, no matter how late it was; there was always something going on that was keeping me awake.

Her impact on my life was profound. Her boldness and faith were contagious.

4

THE CENTER FOR
URBAN THEOLOGICAL STUDIES

Early on in the life of PACS, the board began to discuss the need for continuing ministry training for themselves. None of these pastors had a college degree or had been to seminary. They had attended Manna Bible Institute and gained Bible knowledge there, but they had not received solid theological and ministry training. I was asked to approach Westminster Seminary to see if they would offer classes for these pastors.

I was at first reluctant to do so, because the seminary was very white and had shown no interest in the city. Besides, they were Reformed, while these pastors were all Pentecostals orw Baptists, But because they persisted, I went to the seminary with their request. The seminary delegated the task of meeting with the South Philadelphia pastors to the two systematic theology professors, Norman Shepherd and Robert Stremple. Now I was sure that this wasn't going to work.

The initial meeting was held at the Christian school on a very cold day. The group's leader, the Reverend Eugene Graves, began the meeting with a call to pray—on our knees, on a cold floor, for forty-five minutes. This is not something that Presbyterians do.

And yet, something extraordinary occurred as we prayed. God was binding our hearts as brothers in Christ. Prayer had leveled the ground. When we arose the professors asked, "What would you ask of the seminary?"

It was determined to ask the seminary to offer a series of Saturday Seminars for pastoral leaders in the city. The professors agreed to take the request to the seminary.

In short order, the faculty approved the request. I was asked to be the liaison between the groups. It was pure genius when Dr. Edmund Clowney, the seminary's president, determined that the group of pastors should be the steering committee giving direction to the project.

It was determined to launch the Westminster Saturday Seminar, which offered weekly seminars on assorted topics. The seminars quickly gained traction. Attendance grew rapidly, with up to a hundred pastors attending each Saturday. The breadth of those attending grew quickly, adding Baptists, Methodists (mostly from the African Methodist Episcopal Church), and Mennonites to the initial band of Pentecostals.

In 1973, Dr. Harvie Conn, after having served eight years as a missionary in Korea, joined the faculty of Westminster as Assistant Professor of Apologetics. He was asked to become the liaison between the steering committee and the seminary. I became a member of the steering committee at that time.

Under Conn's leadership, the Saturday Seminars transitioned to become the Westminster Ministerial Institute, a three-year certificate program of biblical, theological, and ministry courses. Enrollment stayed stable during this season, and diversity of theological perspectives among students continued to grow.

THE BIRTH OF CUTS

By 1975 it became clear that another step forward was needed. At that time, all M.Div. programs required a bachelor-level degree for admission. None of the participants had a college degree, so students who completed the program still couldn't attend a seminary degree program. It was thus determined that the program should seek to become a degree-granting college program.

This proved to be a formidable undertaking. The State of Pennsylvania required that all college programs be fully accredited by a Regional accrediting association before they could obtain permission to grant degrees. The state's requirement included an endowment of at least $500,000, eight full-time faculty, and a sufficient library of books to support the course offerings.

I was asked to resume the leadership of the program and begin a search for a fully accredited Christian college in Pennsylvania that would be willing to offer such a program under its auspices. This effort extended over the next three years. None of the Philadelphia-based Christian colleges were interested. After knocking on several institutional doors without success, we seemed to have hit a wall.

In the winter of 1974–75, Geneva College of Beaver Falls, PA planned to hold a dinner for alums and donors in Philadelphia. Dr. Jack White, then Dean of Religious Services, was to represent the college. But there was heavy snow the evening of the dinner, leading him to cancel the event. Instead, he called those who were to have attended, updating them on developments at the college over the phone. One of those he called was my colleague, Wilson Cummings, who was a Geneva graduate. Wilson told Dr. White about the program and the need we had for a college that would partner with us. He agreed to take our request back to the college. In short order, Geneva agreed to sponsor the program.

The biggest challenge was that Geneva College was 340 miles away. The college was unwilling to open a branch campus in Philadelphia, but they were willing to give credit for courses offered provided that the Philadelphia group would raise the funds, hire the staff, and obtain a place out of which to operate. This led to the birth of the Center for Urban Theological Studies (CUTS) in 1978.

I was asked to be the Executive Director. I filled this role until 1994. Including the programs from which CUTS evolved, I worked for CUTS for a total of twenty-six years.

The Bible Institute Movement

During all this institutional searching, I discovered the extensive Bible institute movement taking place in Philadelphia. Bible institutes are schools of adult education that do not grant degrees but provide formal training in ministry and intensive study of the Bible. There were almost one hundred institutes serving the city. The largest were Manna Bible Institute and the Deliverance Evangelistic Bible Institute. Some years later, CUTS was asked by the Pew Charitable Trust to do a survey of these institutes. What I discovered was the majority of them were using the correspondence courses of the then Evangelical Teacher Training Association (ETTA). When I called ETTA it became clear that this was happening. Over time they created a new division to assist in this movement. Sadly, today these institutes have waned. But for a long time, they were the ministry training centers for the urban church.

CUTS's Constitution

Remarkably, a growing group of Philadelphia church leaders and representatives of Westminster Seminary and the regional Reformed churches came together to forge this new training center.

The founding board spent the better part of two years writing a governing constitution for the organization of CUTS. Several key things came out of these discussions.

First, it was determined that the board should be comprised of twelve members, six from the urban steering committee and six from the Reformed community. An even number was chosen so that no one group dominated. If there was a tie vote, discussion would be needed to reach consensus. This proved to be genius. Many major challenges lie ahead.

The elephant in the room proved to be the racial divide. It became quickly obvious that African American church was seen as inferior to the white, Reformed church. This led to many discussions on what the two entities believed and what their practices were. One major hurdle we faced was the issue of whether or not there was such a thing as institutional racism. Two brothers of opposing viewpoints were assigned the task of addressing this question: Dr. Edmund Clowney, then president of Westminster Theological Seminary, and Dr. Carl F. Ellis, then an M.Div student at Westminster who was working part-time at CUTS. Carl contributed greatly to all of the strategic discussions surrounding CUTS's constitution. He subsequently became a leading African American Christian apologist. With great assistance from both Carl and Ed Clowney, these discussions about race led to the writing of the Preamble to the CUTS Constitution and a doctrinal statement, "Foundations for Doing Theology in Ministry." Both of these documents (found in the Appendices) took the issue of race head on, on a foundation of biblical truth.

Another significant discussion was working through the model of raising up leadership. The Black church didn't require a Bachelor's or Master of Divinity degree to become a minister. Apprenticeship was generally required to prepare someone for pastoral ministry, and would sometimes lead to a candidate going on to seminary. With the traditional Reformed churches, these were fundamental for qualifying for ordination and may or may not have included an apprenticeship. We determined that our training would be a biblical-theological model with apprenticeship.

The founding board also discussed the challenge presented by theological differences. The board produced the statement "Learning Together with an Open Bible" (also in the Appendices), which addressed the question of how two diverse theological groups can work together without annihilating one another. It was determined that the faculty of CUTS would include both the Reformed perspective and the broader urban perspective. This became a distinguishing dynamic of the ministry.

The practice of learning together with an open Bible resulted in students realizing the biblical unity of the church. (See Eph. 4:1–3 and 1

Cor. 12:12–27.) It also resulted in racial reconciliation. Several alums have stated that racial reconciliation was achieved without ever talking about it. It just happened from learning together in community with an open Bible.

THE EARLY YEARS OF CUTS

I said that our greatest liability was that Geneva was over 300 miles away. It turned out that Geneva being over 300 miles away was also our greatest asset. This required that we develop key institutional structures ourselves, and we were able to do so in a way that fit CUTS's unique mission and setting. We developed the staff structure, found qualified faculty well-suited to CUTS, and put an appropriate advisory structure in place for guiding the students in their studies.

In those first couple of years, there were three full-time employees and one half-time employee. Our early staff: Michele Black, Carl Ellis, Dave Garnett, and myself.

While I regularly taught courses and advised students, I was also responsible for managing the finances and raising all necessary funds. I also served as an academic dean. Slowly, over the years, we were able to add staff to fill these roles. But my greatest passion remained the development of the curriculum, which over time came to be truly contextualized to the urban context of ministry.

The guidance given to me by George Webber, then president of New York Theological Seminary, was invaluable. He advised that we start with a blank sheet of paper to plan curriculum and a potential student assessment. And so that is what we did. We didn't go to other seminaries' templates of courses and program structure. We built ours from scratch based on our unique demographic. (See Appendix D—The Urban Ministry Leadership Program.)

The Center for Urban Ministerial Education (CUME) in Boston and the Urban Theological Institute (UTI) at Lutheran Seminary in Philadelphia started at the same time as CUTS. Given that the majority of students in our target audience did not go to college, CUTS focused on undergraduate education while the other two focused on graduate and certificate training.

Initially, we offered the B.S. degree in Biblical Studies through Geneva College. This was the same program offered at Geneva College, with the exception that we were allowed to offer courses more relevant to the African

American culture. We believed that the community and cultural context of our students was relevant to our curriculum.

We started with only pastors as students. We assumed that pastors needed to be first because they wouldn't attend with the broader Christian community of church members. Once the first group of pastors finished the program, they wanted the members of their church to get a college education, too. Eventually, pastors were able to take classes alongside their members.

At that time, sixty to seventy percent of Philadelphia Hispanic and African Americans were high school dropouts, meaning that they needed to complete high school to enter college. Fortunately, the US provides a path to a high school diploma called a General Education Diploma (or GED), earned by passing a test of fundamental academic skills. Consequently, forty percent of our initial student body came to us with a GED.

Many students also came without viable writing skills. Consequently, we offered three writing courses to get students up to speed in this area.

Reducing the Cost of an Education

We strove to keep the cost of attending CUTS down to make our programs affordable. To reduce the cost of a college education, we offered four options:

1. ***Credits through testing***. Because so many of our students had attended a three- or four-year Bible institute program, we designed a series of tests to determine the level of knowledge of the student. For two of the tests, Old Testament Introduction and New Testament Introduction, students were awarded three college credits for earning a grade of eighty percent or better.

2. ***Bible institute credit***. Students could also receive two-thirds of a college credit for each of the Bible Institute courses for which they had received a grade of B or A. This, along with credits through testing, allowed the student to earn up to thirty college credits. These credits applied toward a couple of degree-required courses, but most were applied as elective credits.

3. ***Credit for life experience***. Recognizing that our students were already in leadership positions in the church and in their vocations, we developed a way to identify and grant credit for life experience learning. This life learning was documented through a Life and Ministry Experience portfolio.

4. ***The First Year Diploma Program***. Finally, we designed a first-college-year diploma program for ten courses (thirty college credits). This program

was offered at a reduced cost directly by CUTS, with Geneva College granting full credit upon matriculation into the degree program. These courses were: English Composition, Speech, Old Testament Introduction, New Testament Introduction, Foundations of Christian Thought (Christian World & Life View), Developing in Ministry, Sociology, Psychology, plus two additional courses. The tuition for this program was greatly reduced from the normal college program. Through these means the cost of the program was greatly reduced, saving the student $400 per credit in tuition, with the result that students did not need to borrow money for their education.

Over the years, we continually sought innovative ways of keeping the tuition costs low. We used the FAFSA assessment to assess the amount of discretionary income students had to spend on education. Any excess amount was covered by a CUTS grant. It's important to note that CUTS had no reserve funds to cover the cost of these grants. We simply went without the income. This practice was ended shortly after I left. The result: students were expected to take out loans to cover the outstanding amount. In retrospect, I should have sought to raise funds for scholarships. That would have been easier than raising funds for the General Operating Budget.

Distinctives of the Program

A survey of former faculty and students pointed to a number of distinctives of the CUTS program:

Critical thinking. Critical thinking was a requirement in all courses. The students were encouraged to hear and reflect on views other than their own and to apply the learning to their lives. They were also encouraged to test their own assumptions by Scripture.

Before Christ and after Christ dynamic. We operated with the understanding that when a person comes to Christ, life changes dramatically. A person gets motivated to serve Christ, and a growing desire arises to know God's Word. A sense of calling and placement in ministry comes with this.

Doing theology in the context of ministry. This was another key dynamic. Theology is not just learning from the past but also the searching of the Scriptures to address the issues the church is facing at the present time. We taught and utilized Dr. John Frame's (Reformed Theological Seminary, Orlando, FL) definition of theology: "Theology is the application of Scripture by Christians to every area of life." We understood this as a process, as depicted in the following graphic:

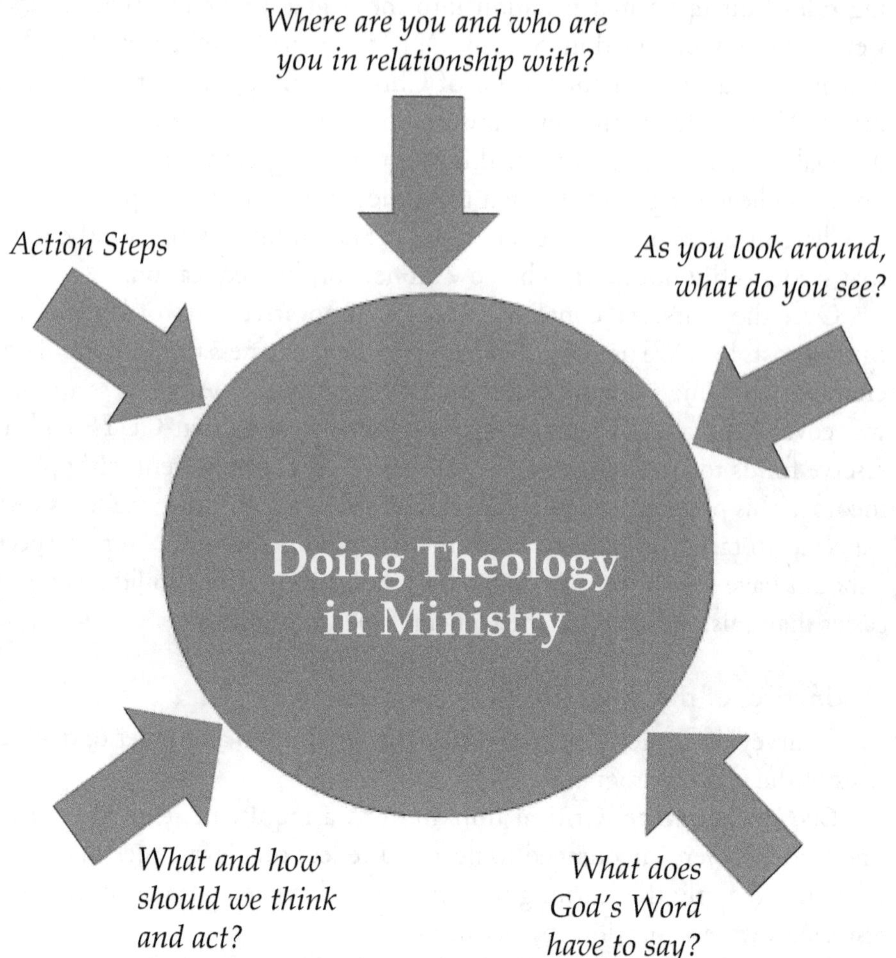

Theology in Ministry

Learning in community. Learning happened in community among the students taking a course and was not individualistic. Frequently, the students were asked to have group discussions and do group projects. Learning to consult and collaborate was a key learning dynamic.

The unity of the church. Along with this was an emphasis on the church as the body of Christ, resulting in a deepening appreciation for the unity of the church. This comes from 1 Corinthians 12:12–27, where we learn that there is one body with many parts, members together. We can never say that I don't need you, nor can we say that you don't need me. By this emphasis, many walls of division in the church were broken down and students were encouraged to embrace one another as brothers and sisters in Christ. Also, racial reconciliation often resulted from this dynamic.

Servant leadership. This submitting to one another demonstrated and enabled servant leadership. We are called to humbly work together for the benefit of all and not to merely exercise authority over each other.

Learning to be disciples making disciples. 2 Timothy 2:2 was a key curriculum dynamic: "And the things you have heard me say in the presence of many witnesses entrust to reliable people who will also be qualified to teach others." Pass on what you have received.

The ministry project. This was the concluding piece of the Urban Ministry Leadership program, and it greatly facilitated the integration of life and ministry.

Graduate degrees. One-third of CUTS graduates went on to earn Master's degrees, primarily the Master of Divinity degree. And a quarter of those completing Master's degrees went on to earn a Doctor of Ministry degree. A few have even earned Ph.D. and/or Ed.D. degrees.

AWARDED THE HONORARY DOCTOR OF DIVINITY DEGREE

I never took the time to work on an academic doctorate. I may have if I had had a computer back in my post-seminary years. But I worked with a manual typewriter until the mid-eighties.

During the later eighties, the Pew Charitable Trust told five Philadelphia-area theological and ministry training schools they had funded in the past that there would be no more grants unless they worked cooperatively at urban ministry. The five were Eastern Baptist Seminary, St. Charles Borromeo Seminary, Westminster Seminary, Lutheran Theological Seminary, and CUTS.

The deans and presidents of these institutions met monthly for discussions around urban ministry. Each year, a different person would be asked to chair the meeting. In the fourth or fifth year, it became my turn. At the first meeting, I began by asking each one to introduce themselves to the group. Every year, there would be at least one or two who were new to their jobs. So, round the table we went. And each one told us their educational background and the topic of their doctoral dissertation as well. When it came back around to me, I called us to take up the business at hand. Immediately, Dr. Manfred Brauch of Eastern Baptist stopped me and said, "You didn't tell us about yourself." I said, "I have a B.A. in history and philosophy from North Park College in Chicago and a Bachelor of Divinity from

Westminster." He leaned back in his chair and said several times, "Really? . . . Really? . . . Really?"

One week later, I received a letter from him telling me that I had been approved by the board of Eastern Baptist to receive the honorary Doctor of Divinity degree. Needless to say, I was floored. I didn't know how I really felt about this. I never introduced myself as "Doctor" or "Reverend." I was always just Bill.

My colleagues of that era also know that I always dressed down wherever I went. This was especially so at CUTS. I never liked neckties. And I rarely wore a suit. Students at CUTS didn't know what to do with this. Almost all the men would wear a suit when they started studies. Eventually, they would come to class wearing gym clothing. They would often ask me why I did this. I said that at CUTS, we come together as family. This was a game-changer and broke down many walls of formality.

My Departure

Over the years of my tenure, we lived on a shoestring. Meeting the biweekly payroll was always a challenge. Nevertheless, we never missed a payroll. A good month was when we began the month with nothing in the bank, we paid all our bills, and we ended with a balance of $0.

Over time, this took a heavy toll on me, resulting in my resignation from the executive position in 1994. I stepped down as Executive Director, but I agreed to stay on for a period to help with the transition, which I did until 1997.

THE CONCLUDING YEARS OF CUTS

In 2011, I returned to CUTS to assist in finding a new educational partner. It was ultimately decided that the new partner would be Lancaster Bible College. My last official act was the adoption of this new program. I confess that in leaving, I had no confidence that either school would follow through on the stipulations of the plan. Indeed, it turned out that neither one followed through.

In 2012, CUTS began to run a budget deficit and needed the help of Lancaster Bible College to bail them out. This resulted in the name being changed to the Lancaster Bible College Program in Philadelphia in 2015. Sadly, the program has ceased being contextualized to the city and its churches since that time.

FRUIT FROM THIS MINISTRY

Over 1,200 Philadelphia church leaders have earned a college degree through the ministry of CUTS.

Over the years, the average student was forty-three years old, fifty percent were men and fifty percent women. The overwhelming majority of students were African American, but they also included small minorities of Anglos, Hispanics, and Koreans. Most were pastors or ministers on the ministerial staff of local churches.

When we began, most African American pastors did not have a college degree. Over the past fifty years that has changed. Because of increased educational opportunities, many now have college degrees. A new educational culture has emerged in the Philadelphia church.

Many new churches were planted, and community ministries were established because of the required ministry projects. By 1990, we had churches all over the city led CUTS graduates.

Over the years of my tenure, the student body grew to 250 students with a staff of eighteen full-time employees, five of which were full-time faculty.

In my final year as executive director (1993–94), the budget of the center was $1.4 million, with $800,000 coming from tuition and $600,000 from contributions and grants.

Testimonial: Dr. Wes Pinnock, Founder/Pastor, True Life Fellowship Church in Philadelphia and CUTS Board Member

I first met Dr. Bill Krispin in the fall of 1974. At the time he was Director of Westminster Ministerial Institute, a leadership training program for urban church ministry. I was then a teacher at the Deliverance Evangelistic Church. Since then, Bill has been a mentor and friend for almost fifty years. This was my first time being exposed to theological training. After graduating from the Institute, a three-year program, the next step in the journey was going through the bachelor's program. As we were going through the Institute program, it became apparent to us that we needed much more training than we were being taught—two hours twice per week. This came about because Bill had formed an Advisory Council made up of himself and five students which helped to arrange the program of the Institute. It was then that Bill reached out through someone at his church who had attended Geneva College to find out if there was a possibility Geneva would offer courses in Philadelphia. This began the Center for Urban Theological Studies. The impact Bill has had on my life and countless others cannot be measured until we all meet in heaven. His leadership was such that until this day his name is synonymous with CUTS. We are thankful he allowed the LORD to use him in this way.

Testimonial: Dr. Jim Petty, CUTS Board Member—Reflections on the Ministry of Bill Krispin

I have known Bill since my first year at Westminster Theological Seminary—1966. Bill was the treasurer of the WTS students dining club—which I promptly joined. I took over as treasurer and was schooled by Bill on how to get the best deals on food from Rotelle's Food Distribution. I was pretty impressed by his resourcefulness—learned on the streets of the near north side of Chicago. I had no idea how much I (a naïve NC native) would be schooled by Bill in the ways of the big city over the next fifty years.

Bill had interned at Tenth Presbyterian Church as a pastoral assistant and gotten involved with youth ministry in South Philadelphia during that time. God put it in Bill's heart (through a woman at Tenth Presbyterian Church) to reach out to children and youth in that community. He finished up his work at Tenth Presbyterian and, in 1967, began to explore moving with his family to South Philly. In June 1968 (I believe), Bill did move his family there as a home missionary with the Orthodox Presbyterian Church—working to plant a church and have a ministry to local youth. What is ironic is that I followed Bill as a pastoral intern at Tenth Presbyterian in the summer of 1967 and served for the next year in the college and career ministry there.

Bill's faith for urban ministry was a great example and motivator for me as I contemplated also moving into a high-crime, quasi-urban neighborhood to start a church on the Penn Campus. Bill was a year or so ahead of me in his ministry, and I found comfort in his rock-solid faith in Christ for his move to South Philly. There was not a lot of obvious overlap in our ministry strategy or cultural context, but just knowing he and Mary were there in a much more difficult situation than I faced helped me navigate the waters of urban living for the first time in my life. Bill was a dynamo of resourcefulness in rehabbing a row house, locating discounted fifty-pound bags of flour and powdered milk, buying sides of beef to freeze, and locating a garden plot we could both use to raise our own food. He was also a master at networking. Just the skills God would use for a lifetime of ministry entrepreneurship for the Kingdom of God.

During the early years of our city ministry, there was little overlap between his work and mine. Both churches had been founded, and we were each hard at work focused on different neighborhoods and different cultures. However, as our children approached school age, the need for their schooling became an issue. Bill and some other urban pastors had started a school in North Philadelphia and planned to open a branch at 52nd and Market Streets—where we were hoping to send our children. Again, Bill introduced me to urban Christian schooling.

That branch school never materialized, and so we decided to begin Spruce Hill Christian School (now The City School) with children from Bill Krispin's church and our church plant in Southwest Philly. Bill's experience, connections to urban leaders, and faith for ministry (in beginning PACS) was an inspiration to us. I had a lot to learn about the urban community, and Bill led the way for me. However, I did not realize I was just beginning my journey of learning and understanding with Bill lighting the way for me and numbers of others in the north suburbs. For me, most of it happened through the Center for Urban Theological Studies (CUTS).

Using all his networking skills, Bill recruited a board for CUTS—balanced between leading urban pastors and those of us who were connected to the Reformed educational establishments (and the Orthodox Presbyterian Church). Many of the city-based early board members were also students at Geneva via CUTS; their ministries thrived in the city, and most earned bachelor's degrees. I can testify that the mostly white Reformed members of the board went through a learning process about the integrity, faith, and wisdom of our urban brothers whom we had never known or even known about. With Bill's relational skills and cultural and biblical insight, mutual trust and understanding grew as we struggled together to guide CUTS through these uncharted waters. I am sure Bill will describe the dynamics of this, but it I can testify that it was one of the highlights of God's work in my opinion.

I believe CUTS worked because of the level of trust and love among a very diverse group of church leaders. I was privileged to serve two stints on the CUTS board from the founding of CUTS in 1978 to the transition to Lancaster Bible College. I can say that the relationships in Christ with the other men on the board were one of the greatest sources of growth in my faith, understanding, and joy in the Lord. Service on the board was difficult from a practical and institutional perspective because what we were doing was unprecedented, but it was one of the great privileges of my life, and

God used Bill Krispin to connect me to these riches. I am deeply thankful to God for that blessing.

From my perspective, Bill was almost like a conduit for ministry relationships between city-based Christians and those in the suburban churches. Both were part of the Body of Christ, but God used Bill to connect hundreds of church leaders. Bill could interpret the city-based cultures to those of us not from the city and as well as interpret the Reformed faith of suburban Christian leaders to city leaders. Because of these relationships, the church in the Philadelphia region is far stronger today than it was when Bill and Mary first moved into 15th and Federal Streets in 1969. In substantial ways, God used Bill as one of his most choice servants to connect the regional body of Christ in the Lord.

The urban church has been built up in the gospel and in ministry through CUTS. My somewhat dated estimate of the number of Christians (just in Philadelphia) sitting under the preaching and ministry of leaders who came through CUTS would add up to over 30,000 each Sunday morning. Because of CUTS, these church leaders have solid theological and ministry training, are better connected to the suburban leaders, and are also influencing those suburban leaders as they struggle with how to lead their churches forward in areas of racial reconciliation, justice ministry, and evangelism.

My prayer is that we all would build on the foundation Bill helped lay. That we would remember the vision Christ has for the church that its leaders would know and love each other. Bill has helped us begin the journey towards that goal. I hope we will remember his witness so that we might continue to realize and enjoy the riches of Christ's body built together in love.

Testimonial: Dr. Sherry Jones, CUTS Faculty

If someone asked me who Bill Krispin is, I would say he is my mentor, my teacher, and my friend. He has helped shape my ministry involvement and focus in the city of Philadelphia. I learned from him how to prepare CUTS students for ministry that was transforming and vital to the body of Christ. One main point I learned from Bill was to be aware of where God is at work and join Him.

I had the privilege to teach a course that Bill wrote on discipleship. I watched students grow in grace and realize that they were called to be interdependent—not independent—in their walk in Christ. It changed their whole perspective on life within and outside of the church. The book changed students' lives and ministry.

As a friend, Bill has always been concerned about my own spiritual maturity. He confronted me, encouraged me, and affirmed me in such a manner I knew I was loved. In my faith tradition, we would call Bill a spiritual father; maybe in other traditions he is a disciple-maker. However you coin it, Bill is a brother after the heart of God.

Testimonial: David Garnett, CUTS Staff—Remembering Bill Krispin

I am David A. Garnett, and I worked at the Center for Urban Theological Studies (CUTS) from 1979 until 2002. As I remember it, in 1979 my pastor Rev. Willie Richardson (Christian Stronghold Baptist Church) asked to meet with me, and in that meeting he told me about a ministry called "CUTS" (Center for Urban Theological Studies) that needed workers, and he thought that I might be a good fit there. I had completed my undergraduate degree at Rutgers University and had been working at the Internal Revenue Service for five years, but I was very much interested in working for a ministry, although I was not a "Reverend." A meeting was arranged for me to meet Rev. William C. Krispin, the Director of CUTS. Pastor Richardson made it clear that I should focus upon assisting Rev. Krispin. After my interview with Rev. Krispin (which I thought went well), I met with Pastor Richardson again, and he made it clear that if I were to be offered a position that I had to remember that I was to assist Rev. Krispin who was the Director of CUTS. One of the things that became clear to me when I met with Rev. Krispin is that this man lived and breathed the ministry and was seriously committed to his family. I was deeply impressed. As it turned out, I was offered a position at CUTS, which I accepted. When I started at CUTS, I had the opportunity to see the incredible work ethic of Bill Krispin. He was involved in everything at CUTS, he also had a wife and children, and he was a preacher!! I was stunned at how he could stay on top of everything. One of the first things that I noticed about Bill Krispin is that he was virtually always at CUTS or at a ministry-related meeting, yet he was married with children. It became clear to me that one way to assist both Bill and the CUTS ministry was to arrange for me to be present at CUTS as much as possible day and evening. (Most of our classes were held on weekday evenings or on Saturday.) To me it was obvious what I should do…Bill was a preacher, he was married, and he had children. On the other hand, I was not a preacher, I was single, and I had no children. I chose to begin spending as much time at CUTS as possible. This would free up some of Bill's time, which blessed

CUTS as Bill focused on the direction of the ministry. During the years that I worked with Bill Krispin at CUTS, I was always deeply impressed with his commitment to his family and to CUTS.

Testimonial: Wilbert Richardson, Pastor and CUTS Board Member— A Wonderful Encounter

In 1976, I was introduced to Reverend Bill Krispin and the Center for Urban Theological Studies (CUTS) by Reverend Paul V. Clark, my pastor and my lifelong friend and mentor, and Reverend Dr. Willie Richardson, a son of Calvary Baptist Church located in North Philadelphia, who encouraged me to meet with Bill to discuss the possibility of joining the CUTS family. I met with Dave Garnett, Bill's assistant, and the rest was history; I began the enrollment process. A truly defining point in my life. After graduating CUTS, Bill and Harvie Conn encouraged me to continue my formal education at Westminster. And by the grace of God, after graduating and sometime later, I became fifth president of CUTS born and raised in North Philadelphia. That's what CUTS was for ordinary people like me. Thanks, Bill, to God is the glory.

Meeting Needs for Urban Education: Bill Krispin has been a gifted resource person in many areas of ministry for anyone whom he encountered for as long as I have known him. Among other areas of ministry, urban education and ministries to plant and grow churches have been those he is noted for—to this present day. I have profited from both. CUTS has been an oasis for local pastors like me who sought higher education. Missionaries, church leaders, and those who just wanted to do theology from a biblical context found a path forward at CUTS. Bill Krispin was the go-to person for those abroad nationally and internationally who desired a chance to do urban ministry.

The CUTS Model: We know there were other great men in Philadelphia and other cities, like Drs. John White, Harvie Conn, Roger and Edna Greenway, and Sam Logan, who partnered with Bill to make CUTS a reality. The "CUTS model" was designed for the disenfranchised and those who had a sincere call to minister in our cities. Many who attended CUTS had full-time jobs, families, and were already doing ministry in their homes and storefronts. CUTS was noted for "meeting you where you are and helping take you to where you wanted to go." The aforementioned statement and fact was coined by one of the CUTS graduates, Dr. Stanley Hearst. Those of us who worked with Bill know him to be modest about accepting credit for birthing such a ministry. But again, thank you Bill, you did it, and many like me have prospered for the work you were called to do. "To God be the glory!"

Testimonial: Dr. Willie Richardson, Founder/Pastor, Christian Stronghold Church

Bill Krispin has been my friend and brother in Christ for over fifty years. I have learned so much from him over our friendship and serving in ministry together. He was always available to lend a listening ear and give biblical direction and advice as I pastored my large congregation. We served on several boards and committees together to help advance the kingdom of God. Bill never wavered in his faith, even during difficult decision-making times in our board meetings. There are several biblical characters that Bill displays, and one character that resembles him the most is Joshua's determination to worship and service God and his people no matter the circumstances. Bill leaves a legacy of being a Bible scholar, leader, and friend.

Testimonial: Tom Tomer

In the late seventies, my pastor, the Rev. Tom Tyson, asked me if I'd be willing to serve on the organizing board of the Center for Urban Theological Studies (CUTS). He gave me a brief history on how the Orthodox Presbyterian Church became involved with CUTS and suggested that I could assist in this endeavor because of my management experience. The organizing board was comprised of equal representation from the urban and reformed churches. The first task of the board was to formulate a constitution that would define the organization. At the time, I assumed that this process wouldn't take more than two or three months, and then my responsibilities would be over. But it became apparent that this organization was more complicated and challenging than I expected. That wasn't because of technical considerations. It was because of how much I needed to learn and appreciate about the church that God established in Philadelphia. During this time on the board, as well as the years that followed, my association with Bill Krispin was encouraging and invaluable.

I knew of Bill Krispin as a minister in our presbytery, but I did not know him personally. That would change later, because after the work on the organizing board had been completed, I had the honor to serve on the operating board until 1995. However, given my background and training, my contribution to the operation of the CUTS organization was minimal. What is significant was the effect that my association with CUTS has had on me. Bill Krispin was the major player in that process. Bill understood the cultural unawareness that can easily characterize people from my ecclesiastical background. Bill was always patient but direct in his counsel and leadership. Moreover, Bill's ability to pull together brothers from theologically diverse communities into an effective organization is a genuine gift from our God. The blessings that accrue from such organizations are incalculable; it's something that cannot be accomplished simply through the management process. I have many fond memories of my association with CUTS. It may seem like a small detail, but one of the most memorable blessings was the welcome I received from my brothers in the black churches. The first consideration always seemed to be, "Does this guy really love Jesus?" They may have been concerned about my theology, but if so, it could be dealt with later. I remember Bill saying, "Our black brothers don't tolerate any 'funny stuff.'" And so, I have a significant debt of gratitude for Bill Krispin and the organization that he led. I received much more from CUTS than I contributed.

I know our great God always accomplishes "all of his purposes" (Isa. 46:10), but he does work through those he has called for that purpose. CUTS happened in the providence of God. But personally, I can't imagine it without Bill.

Testimonial: Celeste Wynn

I have had the good pleasure of knowing Dr. William Krispin for over forty years. I know him as a colleague and a friend. I first met him in a parent/teacher relationship. I taught two of his children, Jonathan and Karen, at the Philadelphia Association of Christian Schools (PACS) in the early 1980s. His children were exceptional students, and he was one of the board directors of our school. He was committed to urban ministry and demonstrated his commitment by living in the neighborhood where the school was located—the Germantown section of Northwest Philadelphia—and enrolling his children in our school.

I worked at PACS for two to three years before returning to university to complete my Master of Education degree. Bill later invited me to teach English courses at the Center for Urban Theological Studies (CUTS) upon the retirement of Dr. Abraham Davis. This appointment began my thirty-five-year relationship with CUTS.

CUTS experienced growing pains, and Bill, the late Dr. Harvey Conn, Pastor Benjamin Smith, Dr. Willie Richardson, and others kept our school going. Their collective commitment and Bill's steadfastness is why CUTS, now known as Lancaster Bible College, still exists today.

During his tenure, Bill remained faithfully committed to the CUTS vision. When he was no longer the Executive Director, he continued to advocate for the faculty, staff, and student body. He, like Nehemiah, remained faithful and dedicated to building CUTS and the mandate to educate urban pastors and provide them with access to undergraduate and graduate degrees through Geneva College and Westminster Theological Seminary. Other graduate schools were later added to our roster, including Biblical, Eastern Baptist, and Lutheran Theological Seminaries. As of this writing, over 100 of our graduates have earned Doctorate degrees at one of these seminaries, to which we say, "To God be the glory!"

The CUTS commitment to urban pastors was open and accessible to Black, Latino, Korean, and urban White pastors. This racial mix opened doors of opportunity for these pastors to communicate with each other and establish relationships, which would not have been possible without the CUTS experience.

In 2011, Dr. Krispin was integral in establishing an agreement with Lancaster Bible College in Lancaster County, Pennsylvania. Lancaster absorbed our school, which was later known as CUTS/LBC, then LBC. The rest is history. Like the Apostle Paul, Dr. Krispin can rightly say, "I have fought the good fight, I have finished the race, I have kept the faith. Now there is in store for me the crown of righteousness, which the Lord, the Righteous Judge, will award to me on that day and not only to me but also to all who have longed for His appearing" (2 Tim. 4:7–8). An accompanying meditation in the NIV Worship Bible says: "Holy and Righteous Father, I want my life and not merely my lips to offer the worship of which You alone are worthy. In view of Your mercy, I offer my body, my whole being, as a living sacrifice. Consume me with Your grace, compel me with Your love. In my living and in my dying may you alone be glorified!"

Testimonial: Rev. Dr. Stanley Hearst, Pastor of the Bethel African American Episcopal Church, Moorestown, NJ

I was born in West Philadelphia, educated in Philadelphia Public Schools and graduated from Overbrook High School in 1971. I earned the Bachelor of Science in Urban Ministry Management in 1991 at CUTS, then the Master of Urban Missiology at Westminster Seminary in 1994, and then the M.Div. degree (1997) and Doctor of Ministry degree at the Eastern Baptist Seminary (now Palmer Seminary) in 1999.

I then served from 1999 to 2016 as Adjunct Professor at the Lancaster Bible College program at CUTS (LBC/CUTS) in Philadelphia.

I am married with three children.

From the student's chair to the adjunct's desk: My journey from an adult learner to an adjunct faculty member began after responding to the call to preach in 1984. I first attending the Deliverance Evangelistic Bible Institute in Philadelphia. However, I needed to find an undergraduate degree program to proceed further, a degree required by the AME church for ordination. I was directed to CUTS led by Dr. Bill Krispin where I enrolled in the undergraduate program in 1986.

During this time Dr. Krispin had begun to develop the BS in Urban Ministry Management that could be completed in 18 months. I was enrolled in the first learning cohort graduating in 1991.

Dr. Krispin taught his courses in such a way that my interest peaked in continuing in higher education. I knew that my writing skills left a lot to be desired and needed.

My interest in teaching as I sat under Dr. Krispin and other excellent teachers. I began to envision myself teaching at CUTS. I had lunch with Professor Celeste Wynn and shared with her that I wanted to teach at CUTS when I finished my doctoral degree which was still a couple of years off. I was blessed to teach at CUTS for 16 years. To God be the glory.

5

THE PILGRIM YEARS (1997–2001)

In 1997, having come to the conclusion that my time at CUTS was over, I began to consider my options. I was asked to consider calls that would take me to Wilmington, Denver, Atlanta, Chicago, and Taiwan. What I learned was that not only do you have to consider if you have a call to a new place; you have to consider, "Are you released from the current ministry to go to a new place?" I really wanted to continue ministry in Philadelphia as I was deeply embedded here in many, many important relationships.

In June 1997, I took the pastorate of Pilgrim Church, a Presbyterian church located in the Manayunk section of Philadelphia. The first year as pastor was filled with drama. I had started with five elders, which quickly dropped to two through one retirement and two stepping down because of confessed sin issues. I had sensed that there was a cloud of spiritual depression hanging over the congregation. There was no joy. Mary and I began to pray that God would show us what was behind this. And he did.

I felt that the congregation had lost a sense of the centrality of the gospel to all that we do. So, I determined to preach a series of sermons from the Gospel of Luke on the theme: Jesus receives sinners who repent and believe.

A real breakthrough occurred in January 1998, when I was informed by the elders that the church annually observed Right-to-Life Sunday. I asked what their practice had been and was told that the pastor always preached a sermon against abortion. I then asked if he had ever preached a sermon on the forgiveness of God to those who have repented and believed the gospel for those who have had an abortion, both the women and the men involved. I was told by one elder that that wasn't necessary because no one at Pilgrim would have an abortion. I knew better. After all, at that time, forty percent of all women in Philadelphia under the age of 40 had had an abortion. But the elders agreed that I could preach on forgiveness for the sin of abortion.

Two days after that sermon, a young woman in the church came to the church office and asked me, "You really believe that the sin of abortion can be forgiven, don't you?" This ultimately led to several women in the church coming forward to confess. There were also husbands who were involved, as well as parents of those who had an abortion. And there were women who had abortions without their husbands knowing it. As we worked through this process of ministry to and discipline of these people, all of them were ultimately repentant, remained in the church, and were restored to fellowship. Joy returned as the gospel took deep root in the church. At the same time, a couple of men came forward to say that they had been sexually molested in their youth by male relatives. Healing came to these as well.

When I started as pastor there, were fifty-six people in regular attendance. Slowly, we began to grow. After four years, we had 120 in regular attendance. We also began a partnership with Leverington Presbyterian Church for the support of a shared youth pastor. This proved to be a great blessing, as the church's youth now were connected to a larger group, affording many new opportunities for fellowship and service.

Then in 1999 I crashed. I had a stroke while vacationing on the beach in North Carolina. After three days, my paralysis had been relieved, but I was left with extreme fatigue. I struggled with severe and debilitating fatigue for six months. I felt that I didn't have the stamina to continue as pastor of Pilgrim. The fatigue abated somewhat after six months. But after two more years, I was still struggling, and I had come to feel that I wasn't adequately serving Pilgrim. This led me to step down as pastor in 2001 and to move in a new direction in ministry.

I am so grateful for the wonderful support of the elders at Pilgrim: Dave Hause, Ralph Angstadt, Bill Whitlock, and Geoff Brock, the last two of whom were added during my tenure. The patience, love, and care they afforded was an enormous blessing. Mary and I remain a part of Pilgrim to this day.

Testimonial: Geoff Brock, Pilgrim Elder—Random Thoughts Regarding Pastor William C. Krispin

When Pastor Krispin arrived in 1997, as with any church, there were a number of unresolved issues, such as personal sin patterns, interpersonal alienation, confusion of roles and responsibilities (role of deacons, for example), etc.

While most people avoid problems and hope they'll self-resolve, Bill isn't wired that way. Here's a typical Bill conversation:

Bill: It's good to see you. How are you?
Geoff: Oh, you don't want to know.
Bill: Of course I do! Tell me about it.

One might liken Bill to a famous chef, always stirring the pot. He challenges your thinking. "Do you see God in this? Do you see Him working?"

This kind of dialog often opened up the proverbial Pandora's Box. For a while, it seemed like someone removed the rug at Pilgrim, and all the things that were hiding underneath sprang forth. These were exciting times. Although some issues were painful, we could see God working to bring recognition, repentance, and restoration in a number of ways. We had hope.

While Germantown is not far from Pilgrim, Bill and Mary decided to move closer, to Roxborough. This was a significant encouragement to the church as Bill was more accessible than our previous pastor who lived farther out. Bill is committed to the city. This also opened up what some may call Bill's Domino Diner ministry. Early morning breakfasts with Bill were precious times, where any subject could be discussed, including the advisability of a steady diet of George's hearty breakfasts. Bill's healthy diet consciousness came years later.

According to my young sons, when Pastor Krispin preached, he explained the Scriptures in an understandable way. Years later, my oldest asked Pastor Krispin, since retired, to officiate his wedding ceremony.

The Krispins were valued members of our home Bible fellowship group for many years. At one point Bill led a study of Ephesians, which created a "wow" moment for two visitors who had never heard the Bible explained in such a manner.

Most people would characterize Bill as even-tempered. Fair enough, but you could get under his skin and bring out the beast, especially if you're both defiant and stupid—stupid is as stupid does (Forrest Gump). Like building a restroom in the sanctuary right behind the pulpit! Really? I hadn't seen Bill get that red-faced angry before or ever since. Sometimes having a sense of humor is the only thing that saves your sanity.

Bill has always been a network guy, a modern Barnabas, encouraging and collaborating with others, many of whom are outside of the typical OPC/PCA orbit. His experience at CUTS and South Philly pastorate helped Pilgrim see that God's Kingdom is broader and more diverse than a somewhat insular church and denomination. Bill brought a number of folks to Pilgrim in the pulpit (e.g., Harvey Conn), as performers (e.g., Ruth Naomi Floyd), as lecturers (e.g., Betty Jean Wolfe), and as members (e.g., Del Deets, Glenn

Wesley Pinnock). The transition from strict use of the Trinity Hymnal to a greater range of worship expressions unlocked many hearts. Pastor Krispin encouraged people to engage in ministry, e.g. supporting Lin Hause to pursue a counseling certificate at CCEF.

When you talk about Bill, you have to talk about Mary. As quiet as she was, she is Bill's human rock. One of the youngsters expressed that he believed that Mary never sinned. Faulty doctrine maybe, but understandable. Those working with Bill quickly learned the value, no, the necessity, of having Mary in the loop to keep Bill properly humble, focused, and regulated.

Testimonial: Dave Hause

I first met Bill Krispin when I was an elder at Pilgrim Church, we were looking for a new Pastor, and I was the head of the Pastor search committee. Shortly into the process, we learned not only was Bill available, but he was very interested. It soon became a "no-brainer," and he rose to the top of the list with his experience, wisdom, and pastoral qualifications.

Bill approached this uncertain congregation with new enthusiasm, vitality, and purpose. I distinctly recall him going from house to house, visiting each member and regular attender of the church.

On more than one occasion, I had the privilege of going with him and hearing his compelling testimony about growing up in Chicago and all the challenges that came with that, including the poverty and "sirens in the night" that haunted him.

As Pastor of Pilgrim church from 1997 to 2001, Bill had an enormous impact on my life personally and as an elder in the church. Bill is a man of integrity, honesty, and persistence to "dig in" to the hard stuff that was going on in the church and in my personal life.

At the time we were a congregation in a "spiritual depression" and he graciously taught us from Isaiah 61. He encouraged us to "be called oaks of righteousness, a planting of the Lord for the display of his splendor." All by the grace and power of Jesus Christ. (It's worth the time to read the entire chapter.)

He encouraged me to first be a good husband and father, to "Watch your life and doctrine closely. Persevere in them, because if you do, you will save both yourself and your hearers." From First Timothy 4:16. I needed to hear this!

In addition, Bill always encouraged us, and still does, to think "outside of the box" while still maintaining obedience and faithfulness to Christ.

He encouraged me as a leader and to also use my musical gifts to play the guitar (unheard of at the time, ha!) to lead the worship team, implementing both contemporary and traditional songs and hymns, with sound gospel-centered lyrics.

He was able to see special gifts in my then wife Lin, moving her to women's ministry and a degree in counseling at CCEF. Naturally that impacted me as well.

Lin was diagnosed with cancer in early 2004 and lost the six-month battle. It was a real roller-coaster ride. Many people were very, very helpful along the way, but (as I recall) Bill was the only one who lovingly and courageously sat me down late in the process and said, "Dave, this may not turn out the way you are hoping. With God's help, you need to prepare yourself" . . . hard words to hear at that time!

A lot has happened since that time. Bill has helped Mimi (my current wife) and I adjust and prepare for re-marriage in 2011, advising, counseling, and performing our wedding ceremony. Bill continues to be a friend to both Mimi and me, always ready for a visit from us and willing to listen, care, and give wise advice.

It is remarkable how he has persevered through some difficult health issues, never giving up! Bill, there are no words to adequately express the impact you have made on our lives and the appreciation and respect we have for you! I appreciate that you are always willing to admit your own shortcomings and sins.

Thank you for the opportunity to put these thoughts down. To God be the praise for intervening in your life and molding you into the husband, father, friend, advisor/counselor, and mentor that you have become.

Testimonial: Monica Bianco

> They will be called oaks of righteousness,
>> a planting of the Lord
>> for the display of his splendor.
>
> (Isa. 61:3)

Isaiah 61 was the first sermon Bill preached as our pastor at Pilgrim Church. It later was the last sermon he preached as our pastor—"Oaks of Righteousness." When I read that verse, I can see an oak tree, strong and tall, bending when it needed to lean towards the sun. Thriving even after being afflicted by weather and disease. We are oak trees, planted by the Lord to display his glory. We are the branches, and Christ is the root.

Bill's ministry at Pilgrim caused me to see how the Lord sees me. How I am viewed in his eyes. I learned to see myself, not with the world's view, but with the Lord's. That I am precious to Him, dearly loved and treasured. That Jesus said I am worth dying for. I discovered and embraced the gifts God gave me. Gifts that are meant for His honor and glory, not my own. To serve with my whole heart, with all that I am. I am a child of God, by His grace.

Thank you, Jesus.

Bill's sermons offered a new jewel and new treasure to uncover. Those sermons revealed unrepentant sin, new biblical knowledge, and a desire to know Christ more. This is when I became "a sermon junkie." I had this new love of sermons. I learned to unpack them, review notes, and dig deeper into the Scriptures. I was finding a new desire for God's word. All the while, being challenged to try new things, take on new tasks. "Teach Sunday School? Are you sure I'm qualified?" I asked. Oh, how I fell in love with teaching those kids and seeing the lightbulbs go on inside their heads. The Spirit at work in those little hearts. Hearing them repeat words from the sermon still brings tears to my eyes: "Jesus came to be three things, a Prophet, a Priest, and King." God was using Bill's words to reach these little ones too. It was a circle of blessings, one to another, to another. We recognized that we are all connected to one another and that we need each other. We rejoiced, struggled, and cried together, always having hope in our pilgrimage together, eyes fixed on Jesus.

With Bill's guidance and support we became a church that truly loves to worship together. To go boldly, persistently, shamelessly to the Lord, in prayer and in song. We do this with confidence, knowing He will meet us there. Honoring the significance of the sabbath day, a day of celebration for our deliverance from sin. Knowing that this is just a glimpse of what heaven will one day be like.

Bill was (and continues to be) a precious gift that I will forever be thankful for. He was the pastor who God placed in my life at a time when I heard God say, "Monica, you are mine and I love you." I was the first new member of Pilgrim in the Bill Krispin era. (I think that makes me his favorite.) I carry a lot of Bill's words in my heart. These reminders pop up and comfort me, encourage me, and convict me. I love Bill and I know that he (and Mary) love me.

I wish I had the skill to adequately express what Bill's time as our Under-Shepherd at Pilgrim meant to me and our church. But I can say this, God changed us, and it was good.

6

THE CITYNET YEARS (2001–2007)

In 2001, we started CityNet with the New Life network of churches. The initial vision for CityNet was to establish a network of churches in Philadelphia for the purpose of seeing new churches planted that would reach the unreached populations of Philadelphia. We began with two church plants: Rock of Israel in the Red Lion area of Northeast Philadelphia and liberti church in the Fairmount section of Philadelphia. Rock of Israel began under the leadership of Ilya Lizorkin. It is a Russian-speaking church, made up of people from several sections of the former Soviet Union. Liberti began under the leadership of Geoff Bradford and Steve Huber with the goal of reaching the emerging generation of urban Philadelphia. This church quickly grew into two congregations: liberti Fairmount under Geoff Bradford and liberti Northern Liberties under Steve Huber. Today, there are a number of congregations of the liberti network scattered across the Delaware Valley and one as far away as Tampa, FL. Only a few of the liberti churches are affiliated with the Presbyterian Church in America; others are affiliated with the Reformed Church in America, and still others are independent. Missional core values are what unite these churches.

The following testimonial gives an excellent example of the impact of CityNet during those early years.

TESTIMONIAL: BRUCE FINN, RETIRED DIRECTOR OF THE PHILADELPHIA CHURCH PLANTING PARTNERSHIP OF THE PCA

And the things you have heard me say in the presence of many witnesses entrust to reliable people who will also be qualified to teach others. (2 Tim. 2:2)

The Apostle Paul's admonition to his younger ministry partner Timothy expresses well the relationship I have enjoyed with Bill Krispin. Like Paul to Timothy, Bill taught, trained, and equipped me for ministry with the expectation that I would equip others to do the same. I call Bill my mentor. As I say this, however, I acknowledge I am among dozens of men who would say the same. Bill is a mentor of mentors, reproducing himself and his ideas in many over the years. In this brief tribute, I will try to summarize the many ways that Bill has influenced me and do so in a way that I hope will bring glory to the One we have served together: Jesus Christ.

Our Meeting

I met Bill Krispin in 2000 at a meeting of the New Life Church Planting Network, soon to be renamed CityNet. I don't specifically remember the exact moment we met, but I'm certain it happened in conjunction with our mutual interest in church planting in the metro Philadelphia area. By that time, I had planted a church in Bucks County, and I was serving as the Chairman of the Church Planting Committee of the Philadelphia Presbytery of the PCA. Because of my service to the Presbytery, I was very much aware of the development of the New Life Church Planting Network. And I was a fan.

I believed that we needed more churches planted in Philadelphia, reaching more people in more places, and planting even more churches together. I was a cheerleader and advocate for the network among other members of presbytery who questioned the need and motivations for it. John Julien and Ron Lutz were both members of the Church Planting Committee in addition to serving as pastors of New Life churches. They had their hands in both pots. That's how I got to know them, they got to know me, and we learned that we shared a common vision for mission in the city. So, when the New Life Church Planting Network called Bill Krispin to be their first Director/Coordinator, he and I were introduced.

At first, I was little more than another face in the crowd at CityNet. I attended as many of the early meetings of CityNet as possible—as a representative of Presbytery, but much more because of my passion for church planting. And I remember Bill and other leaders welcoming me and including me.

The Leaders Forum

Eventually, CityNet began to offer meetings called CityNet Leaders Forum, a monthly gathering of various ministry leaders in and around the city. These forums served several purposes. First, they became connecting points where people from various denominations and networks met and built relationships. Secondly, they equipped pastors, planters, and leaders for outward facing gospel mission. Thirdly, they inspired leaders with a vision that we could accomplish more together than we could ever accomplish separately. Eventually, I came to discover that these three purposes were an expression of Bill Krispin's heart, to see one church on mission together in the city.

There came a time when I was invited into a more inner circle of CityNet and its leadership. I was asked to attend meetings with those who represented various sectors of CityNet's priorities: church planting, pastoral training (or LAMP—Leadership and Ministry Preparation) , mercy ministry (or MercyNet, which included legal help for those who couldn't afford it (or LegalNet)), just to name a few. Of course, these meetings gave me more and greater access to Bill Krispin and his ideas about how ministry should be done. I was like a kid in a candy store. I benefitted greatly from being in the room with Bill and just listening to his guidance on a wide range of topics. I felt a deep and growing connection with Bill as I related to his ideas, and I found that his leadership was inspirational to me. Meanwhile, I continued to pastor the church I had planted in Bucks County, and I continued to serve as Chairman of the Church Planting Team of Philadelphia Presbytery. More and more, however, my heart was drawn toward the possibility of leaving my congregation in the hands of another and planting a new church.

As I began to pray, think, and search through the possibilities of where to plant a church, there was no one who was better qualified to help me than Bill Krispin. As I got to know him, I came to realize that Bill has an extraordinary knowledge of the region and a seemingly endless list of contacts. I was amazed that such a gifted person as Bill was willing to spend time with me on this journey to discover what God had for my future. Quite frankly, Bill took me under his wing, and we began to take numerous car trips together, specifically looking at the Route 202 corridor for potential places to plant. Bill introduced me to several friends who lived, worked, or did ministry along that corridor, each time seeking their insight, wisdom, and advice about our search. The car rides to and from the western suburbs were filled with conversation about the history, development, demographics, and unique characteristics of various places along Rt. 202. Eventually, Bill helped me draw a missional map of the Route 202 corridor, indicating several key locations where a new and strategic church might be planted. It was during this period that I really got to know Bill Krispin, and Bill got to know me.

CityNet and the Partnership

At that same time, the Philadelphia Presbytery was growing and going through some changes. The presbytery was quite large, stretching from the Pennsylvania-Delaware border in the south to the Pennsylvania-New York border in the north, including metropolitan Philadelphia, the Lehigh Valley, and the Scranton-Wilkes Barre area. The Presbytery had appointed a special committee to consider dividing into two smaller presbyteries. From Bill's and my vantage point, there were two main motivations for this division. The first and most obvious motive was convenience: members just didn't like having to drive so far to attend a presbytery meeting. The second and more secret motive was relational: some members of presbytery hoped that a division would separate them from those they often disagree with about presbytery business. Bill and I didn't find either of these motivations very compelling. And we believed that the recommendation coming from the special committee to divide the presbytery in two by using the PA Turnpike as the border was misguided.

I remember Bill saying that if he and I didn't come up with a better idea, the presbytery was likely to accept the committee's proposal. That's where the missional map of Route 202 came into play. In the weeks that followed, Bill and I expanded the map to include the entire presbytery. We generously applied the concept of an "edge city," an idea Bill had learned from a book by the same name. An edge city is a suburban city, a city outside the city, a central place in the shadow of a big city around which people in the suburbs live, work, shop, play, and worship. King of Prussia was one of the first edge cities in America, and it became a model for many edge cities across the country and around Philadelphia. Within a short period of time, Bill and I had developed a drastically different plan for the presbytery, not based on convenience or avoidance, but based on mission.

Our plan, which was mostly Bill's, had four related components. First, we proposed that the Philadelphia Presbytery divide—or "multiply"—into three new presbyteries, each representing a subsection of the connected mission field of the Greater Philadelphia region. One was a presbytery whose borders were essentially the city limits, which would keep the title "Philadelphia Presbytery" and concern itself with planting urban churches. A new "Philadelphia Metro West Presbytery" would focus on church planting in the western suburbs, including the Blue Route and Route 202 corridors. And the third new presbytery was called "Eastern Pennsylvania Presbytery," stretching from the northern suburbs of Philadelphia, north through the

Lehigh Valley, all the way to the PA-New York border. The second component of our proposal was to form a partnership for cooperation in church planting that connected the three new presbyteries and included the New Jersey Presbytery because of its strategic missional relationship to Philadelphia and the region. The third component of the proposal recommended the establishment of a new ministry position: Church Planting Coordinator of what was called "Metro Philadelphia Church Planting Partnership." And the fourth component recommended that I, Bruce Finn, be called to serve as Coordinator. In time, each of these four recommendations were approved by the Presbytery.

Bill Krispin's vision for mission and church planting in Philadelphia changed my life dramatically. During our times in the car together and after many discussions in between, Bill was the first to see my unique gifts and calling from God. At some point in time in our conversations, Bill said, "Bruce, I don't think you should plant another church. I think you should help others plant churches one after the other." Bill saw in me what I've come to describe as an "apostolic calling"; not with a capitol "A," but a small one. This is someone whose gifts are best suited to serve the broader Church of Jesus, and not just one congregation. And while Bill's assessment of my gifts rang true to me, and it explained why I was always a bit unsettled in pastoral ministry, it was revolutionary to me. It changed the way I thought about myself and my future, and, ultimately, it changed the direction of my life. I was elected unanimously by Philadelphia and New Jersey Presbyteries as the founding Coordinator of Metro Philadelphia Church Planting Partnership. I served in that role for 13 years. They were the happiest and most satisfying years of my life in ministry. I felt like I was in the sweet spot of where God wanted me to serve.

Over the next thirteen years, CityNet and the Church Planting Partnership of Presbyteries grew side by side, the Partnership specifically serving the Presbyteries and CityNet serving a much broader coalition of pastors, churches, denominations, and networks. I think it's fair to say that the Metro Philadelphia Church Planting Partnership would not have happened apart from the leadership of Bill Krispin and the momentum of CityNet. In a way, the existence of CityNet alongside the Presbytery made the presbytery jealous in a godly sense to see more churches planted in more places around the region. As members of the presbytery saw the fruit of mission that CityNet produced, more and more members were hungry to see this kind of fruit happen in the PCA.

The Leaders Forum Expands into the Church Planting Connection

During my time of service as the Church Planting Coordinator, I tried to create an atmosphere in which church planters and church planting would prosper. I consulted with churches about their church planting ideas and plans. I coached several church planters through the seasons of their church planting experience. I raised some money and directed it to church planters and their work. I reproduced an Assessment Center in Philadelphia for Philadelphia church planter prospects, the first copy of its kind in the PCA. And I created and hosted a monthly gathering for church planters, first called "Church Planter Community," then the "Church Planting Connection"—an opportunity for church planters in a variety of differing situations to gather, where they could meet, learn from each other, receive training targeted to their needs, and be encouraged in the hard work they were doing. In each of these initiatives, I benefitted from the wisdom, advice, and counsel of Bill Krispin whose vision and values shaped me and shaped everything I did. For months and years, we continued to meet one-on-one to talk through all that was happening and how we could do everything in the most collaborative way.

Church Planting Consulting

One thing that I particularly enjoyed was how Bill and I were frequently asked to do presentations together about matters related to church planting. We were asked to talk about edge cities, how to determine next best places to plant, the competencies of a church planter, how to analyze the mission field of your church, how to form a network, and specifically how to form a partnership of presbyteries for the sake of church planting. All these presentations were prepared in the same way. I would sit in a room with Bill, ask him questions, listen to his answers, and put those answers on PowerPoint Slides with maps, pictures, lists, and process diagrams—from Bill's mind to a PowerPoint. Then, Bill and I would take turns making the presentation, I doing the play-by-play and Bill adding the color commentary. We had fun with this back-and-forth kind of talk. I was honored that Bill shared the platform with me. And, in this way, he contributed greatly to the credibility I acquired as a church planting leader.

Things I Admire about Bill Krispin

As I had the privilege to know Bill through the many conversations and collaboration over the years, I have come to admire him for a long list of unique convictions or competencies he possesses. I have chosen to list a few with a brief explanation of why each was valuable to me.

His knowledge and insight about Philadelphia and Philadelphians. In his book, *The Tipping Point*, Malcolm Gladwell lists three different kinds of people who are necessary to make a thought, idea, or trend go viral or become epidemic. One is what Gladwell calls a "maven," someone who possesses a vast and extraordinary knowledge of a specific subject matter. Another Gladwell calls a "connector," someone who has an extraordinary network of personal contacts and relationships. The third Gladwell calls a "salesman," someone who has an above-average ability to persuade others. Together these three kinds of people can make an idea (or disease) spread exponentially. Bill Krispin is two out of three.

First, Bill is a maven of Philadelphia. I often tell people that Bill Krispin knows Philadelphia better than the mayor. He knows every neighborhood in this city of neighborhoods. He has traveled up and down almost every street on foot or by car. He has studied the history of the city and has a personal collection of maps and charts from past decades. He has lived and listened to the story of the city as told by many of its people in various layers of the city's society. If I needed to know something about Philadelphia, I only needed to turn to my mentor and friend to find the answer. Bill is a walking encyclopedia of the City of Brotherly Love.

His extraordinary network of personal relationships and ministry connections. As if that weren't enough, Bill is not just a maven, he is also a connector, with a vast number of personal relationships collected from years of relationally driven ministry in the city. If I need to know something or someone in Philadelphia, that's a one-stop shop with a quick phone call to Bill. I am amazed at how many people Bill knows, how many leaders Bill has impacted, how many churches Bill has visited, and how many contacts Bill has. If Bill got the flu, before long it would be a city-wide epidemic. I have been inspired by Bill's example to meet more people, learn their stories, and remember them as a part of the network of souls that make Philadelphia such an interesting place to do ministry. He's not just a living encyclopedia, he's a walking phone book.

His absolute commitment to the importance of place. Bill deeply believes in the importance of place—that is, that a pastor and a church ought to be committed to the unique community in which God has placed them and they ought to study it continuously to understand trends and changes that offer opportunities for ministry. Bill would often lament that many pastors of city churches moved out of the city to the suburbs, tacitly giving permission for their members to do the same. For Bill, this was an abandonment of the mission field which created "commuter churches," whose people no longer lived in, understood, or really cared about the neighborhood around the church. Bill sought to reverse this misguided trend by encouraging church planters to live in the community to which they are called to serve. And Bill was a good model of this himself, as he and Mary lived in the city through his many years of ministry there. Place matters.

His vision of one Church and one mission in Philadelphia. One of Bill's favorite teachings has to do with the fact that God has established only one church for the city: the Church of Philadelphia, which has many different parts and expressions, but only one mission together. You can't be around Bill very long before you hear his heart conviction on this matter. He teaches churches and pastors that they each are a part of something greater than themselves and that they can accomplish far more by working together with their neighbors than they ever could alone. One of the main accomplishments of CityNet during the peak of its influence on city ministry was how it brought church leaders together from various denominations, networks, and connections. Those who attended CityNet's Leaders Forum met people they would not otherwise have met. And it nurtured relationships and partnerships in ministry that would not have happened otherwise. The fruit of Bill's efforts in this regard is impossible to measure, since most of these connections happened organically and not through the top-down direction of an institution.

"Collaboration" is Bill Krispin's middle name. I experienced this personally in the ways that Bill worked with me through the Church Planting Partnership. But Bill was forever encouraging pastors and churches to grow in their awareness of others around them and to pursue opportunities to reach and serve their community together. Bill believes that denominationalism and division has hurt the reputation of Jesus among unbelievers. He believes that collaboration and partnerships show off the unity of the Church in ways that are attractive and compelling.

One specific way that Bill's teaching impacted me was how I initiated the monthly gatherings for church planters, or Church Planter Community. Of course, my priority was to provide a rich, encouraging, and enriching environment in which my church planters in the PCA would feel supported in their work. But Bill taught me that a rich environment for PCA planters had to include planters from other networks. Otherwise, it would not be rich. From the start and throughout the many years during which I produced Church Planter Community, I always included non-PCA planters and tried my best to include non-PCA leaders at the highest level of planning and implementation of these gatherings. For many years, I partnered equally with a Southern Baptist leader. For many more years, I partnered equally with a leader from the Christian and Missionary Alliance. And for what turned out to be my final year of leadership over Church Planter Community, I partnered equally with leaders from Liberti, Christian and Missionary Alliance, Assemblies of God, the Epiphany Network of Churches, Southern Baptist and, of course, the Presbyterian Church in America. All were relationships I had because of Bill.

His passion for racial reconciliation in the Church. This list of admired traits would not be complete without mention of Bill Krispin's passion for racial reconciliation in the Church. To be honest, as someone who has spent my entire life growing up and doing ministry in the suburbs, the issue of racial reconciliation was not really on my radar, until I met Bill. Bill introduced me to the first black pastors I ever met, including Hal Hopkins, Eric Lambert, and Lawrence Chiles. Bill told me the story of race relations in the city, saying that racial segregation in the Church was invented in Philadelphia. Bill helped me understand the racial divide in the church of the city and the deep distrust of white churches and pastors caused by decades of broken promises. Eventually, I met Eric Mason and Doug Logan through Epiphany Fellowship, two men who represented a next generation of black leadership of the church in Philadelphia. Bill taught me almost everything I know about the black church in Philadelphia. Everything else I know I learned from Doug Logan, who has become a close friend over the years. I've heard it said that no white man is more welcome in the black church of Philadelphia more than Bill Krispin. And I believe it. I have seen how Bill was received by the leadership of Partners in Harvest/ Harvest Fellowship, a ministerium of black pastors in the city. Bill has worked tirelessly to rebuild broken trust, initiate collaboration between black, white, and Hispanic pastors, submit himself to black leaders in appropriate ways, and initiate conversations in which mutual understanding and respect can grow. You would be hard-pressed to find any white man who has worked harder at racial reconciliation in the Church of Philadelphia than Bill Krispin. His efforts in this regard will be a lasting legacy of Bill's work, bringing great glory to God and impacting the next generation of church leaders, black and white.

Final Tribute

It is a pleasure for me to write this tribute in honor of Bill Krispin, my mentor, my friend, my brother. Bill has been a spiritual father to me, one whose love, encouragement and support I have felt over the years. In ministry, Bill's is the voice I hear inside my head, shaping the way I see the Church, informing my own teaching and preaching, and influencing how I train and disciple others. He is a mentor who has produced mentors who reproduce mentors, whose Christian life will have an impact for God's Kingdom for generations to come.

7

THE LAMP PROGRAM

During the middle years of my tenure with CityNet, I saw the need for leadership development. There were many pastors and people desiring to start new churches but were not particularly interested in doing formal M.Div. studies. Consequently, I developed a ten-course program of ministry and theological studies. This was offered as a learning cohort of students who took all the courses together and in the prescribed sequence.

Because I was already fully committed to other aspects of ministry through CityNet, I determined to find someone who could assume the leadership for the program. This led me to Mark Sarracino, who had served as a missionary in Italy. Together we developed and launched this program.

TESTIMONIAL: DONNY CHO, PASTOR, METRO CHURCH— PERSONAL TRIBUTE TO DR. WILLIAM KRISPIN

I grew up without a father; my father was brutally murdered when I was a child, and as I grew into my university years, through graduate studies, and into my professional career—long before I even considered going into vocational ministry—I could practically feel the effects of not having a father in my life; it was that palpable.

A child without a father faces headwinds and barriers in many dimensions of his life that cannot be addressed no matter how faithful one's mother may be. Every modern cultural giant in our world today—folks like Michael Jordan or Tiger Woods—refers to the significant roles that their fathers played in their lives. Male role models, as a result, have been incredibly important to me; such is the importance of "spiritual fathers" who, knowingly or not, helped to usher, push, inspire, or motivate me by acting as men on the metaphorical mountaintop, who are able to guide me when I'm in the valley. You observe, emulate, listen to, learn from, and follow their example every bit as much as their fatherly, biblical counsel. This was Bill Krispin to me.

Bill was a church-planting titan who shaped the likes of fruitful ministers over decades. His profound perspective of the city, his heart for the poor, and his eye toward the shifting cultural, racial, socioeconomic, historical, and religious landscapes of the urban and city contexts influenced the likes of the late Timothy Keller among church planters all over the country, along with many others.

To this day, I don't personally know anyone else in my life who has had such immense cross-cultural influence in the ministry world. Dr. Krispin is embraced by Black, Brown, White, and Asian—and almost equally; in fact, he is often more comfortable among non-Anglo church leaders than among Anglos from the Presbyterian denominations he ministered in. How many other Caucasian Presbyterian male leaders do you know who have as much influence cross-culturally as Bill Krispin has enjoyed over the past 20 years? As I write today, Dr. Krispin teaches seminary students in China, mentors Hispanic church leaders on the East Coast, is regarded as a personal advisor to Black pastors all over the City of Philadelphia, serves as a mentor to many Asian ministers, all the while regarding himself a retired pastor in the Presbyterian Church in America denomination. The answer to the question above is, "No one." There is not a single person with that kind of personal influence over so many different types of people in ministry.

But I regard him as one of my "spiritual fathers." He introduced me to the "science" of church planting and simultaneously opened me up to a deep love for the city. He opened up opportunities for me to study, learn, gain experience, and develop as a church planter. He demonstrated the importance of mentoring people along their spiritual journeys. He showed me the critical building blocks of a healthy church and healthy pastoring. He also taught me the importance of gospel character and humility, what it means to be a good father, the makings of a good and faithful husband, and the vital importance of curiosity and steadfastness in life and ministry through every valley of life. I am five feet, seven inches tall; when I first met him at a church conference in 2002, Dr. Krispin was a larger-than-life, vibrant man who towered over me; I am amazed, looking back, at the men with whom I've crossed paths—titans of our ministry era—and Bill Krispin was figuratively among the tallest of them.

A Rebel with a Cause

Dr. Krispin came from Chicago and moved to Philadelphia to pursue seminary studies. A rebel at heart, Bill has always challenged the "status quo" ever since his childhood days. One of his greatest qualities, even in his now old age, is his curiosity. He just couldn't accept things as they were—not back then as a child, and not today. Men like that tend to create "wrinkles" in organizations and churches, but you couldn't "shush" Bill Krispin. His curiosities and passions would compel him to seek new and better solutions to anything he laid his hands on, and he wouldn't be stopped by convention or mere tradition. The Lord has it so that men like Dr. Krispin—transformed by the gospel of Jesus Christ—could successfully shape church-planting and ministry for half a century; as the saying goes from the liberal activist-poet Tuli Kupferberg, "When patterns are broken, new worlds emerge." Bill Krispin certainly broke old, fruitless patterns, while shaping the new worlds that emerged.

Church Planting as a "Science"

I recall a time when I was a part of the Philadelphia Presbytery of the Presbyterian Church in America (PCA). Dr. Krispin was asked to provide a seminar (he was in his sixties then) to the Church Planting Committee regarding his view of church-planting today. The PCA, well-known for its commitment to doctrinal integrity, is not known to be a strong church planting denomination, but Bill is way ahead of his time. He began his hour-long discourse with a history of church planting in the Philadelphia area, followed by some of the modern missteps that churches tend to make in planting churches. An example could be seen in how church plant locations are often determined; from his analysis, churches are too pragmatic and historically tied to planting in locales that are now obsolete compared to where the newer generations of people targeted by those church plants reside. The idea is to plant where people are headed, not where they are today. It blew my mind. As a marketing strategist for the better part of two decades, I had never heard this kind of dialogue from a church planter before—or anyone outside of the secular workspace. Bill had reams of data to prove his point: where people resided in the 1960s to where the next few generations migrated into the 2000s. Bill referred to a map of potential areas where a church could thrive among the new generation—many of whom are "dechurched," church-less, or unchurched today.

It was this kind of out-of-the-box thinking that Bill himself regarded as common sense that was frequent among our conversations over the twenty-plus years that I have known him. Church planting was about more than having a burden to do ministry among an unreached people group; it was about looking at data, people-watching, performing contextual and cultural assessments, and prayerfully charting one's journey of ministry in a manner that honored the Lord.

A Renaissance Man

Geniuses may be great at a few things but are knowledgeable in many things. It makes sense, since knowledge and experience tend to feed one's cross-functional expertise. In other words, in order to excel at something, you need to apply the knowledge and experience you've gained from other interests. For example, Billy Beane, the General Manager for the Oakland A's, became famous for his Moneyball approach to building baseball teams, which led to a biographical account of his literally game-changing journey; today, managers in all sports franchises and the corporate world through Wall Street refer to Billy Beane's understanding and use of performance data and analytics. Good leaders learn from the philosophies of people outside their world; their curiosity extends into personal hobbies, interests, and life. Bill was like that. For hours at a time, we'd discuss Malcolm Gladwell's theories of first impressions in Blink or the deferential culture of Koreans and Brazilians which was highlighted in The Outliers. One time, he spent an hour educating me on the conducting genius of a few different versions of G.F. Handel's Messiah; I was amazed by his understanding of this classical masterpiece. He was also a huge Chicago Cubs fan, so as baseball fans, we'd chat at length about the Chicago Cubs, Wrigley Field, and overcoming the "curse" of both the Cubs and Red Sox. He has a profound love for maps; the man possessed some of the oldest authentic maps of the City of Philadelphia that I had ever seen. Of course, he was very well read; we would chat for hours about W.E. Deming's contributions to business and society, and I recall introducing him to Peter Senge's The Fifth Discipline, which he finished by the next time we met.

I remember years ago reading an article about the number of industries and disciplines that have been revolutionized by the late Apple founder, Steve Jobs. When I think of Bill Krispin, I can also recount the many ministerial spheres he shaped. He founded the Center for Urban Theological Studies (CUTS) in Philadelphia in the 1970s; at a time when so many seminaries were retreating to the suburban landscape, CUTS offered more affordable theological training to urban and city-focused ministers—particularly Black and Hispanic pastors in the inner city. Before the PCA denomination really gained an official foothold in Philadelphia, Bill served as the Executive Director of CityNet in the early 2000s—which helped to launch multiple churches (and downstream networks) during its peak years, almost serving as a blueprint for church planting in the Philadelphia area among Presbyterians. He did it again with LAMP Philly (Leadership and Ministry Preparation), providing a seminary M.Div equivalent to those training for ministry in the mid-2000s. He started in ministry in Philadelphia by leading a Christian camp for children and youth in South Philly—out of his own home. He founded Common Grace in the 2000s as a ministry to support church planters with data and analytics research. Long before the political polarization within the church in the wake of COVID-19 and the death of George Floyd, Bill Krispin was spiritually fathering dozens of men from African American, Hispanic, and Asian churches throughout Philadelphia; the man fathers spiritual sons of all tribes. He was a great contributor and educator at a seminary in China since the 2010s, likely paving the way for other church-planting organizations. Authors and scholars from the 1960s through our modern times reference him in their books and other works as a trailblazer in urban education, pastoral ministry, and church planting. Part of Bill's legacy is as an innovator and pioneer in urban ministry and training.

A Foundation of Faith and Faithfulness

It is easy to forget that men like Bill Krispin ever get discouraged, but they do. I'd venture to say that men like Bill face greater discouragement than most. For one, Bill Krispin ministered among the last, least, and lost—the poor and urban communities; ministry in these parts doesn't often receive sufficient attention nor funding. Second, if you read any of the above, Bill was ahead of his years; today, we celebrate him. Today. I imagine thirty-to-fifty years prior, Bill's philosophy of ministry was likely considered risky and difficult to envision. How does one endure discouragement, even opposition, while simultaneously battling the temptation to fight or withdraw from the naysayers?

Dr. Krispin taught me that one's steadfastness and faithfulness in ministry must always be anchored deeply to a personal Jesus, centered around the "already" reality and eschatological "not yet" hope of the gospel. As a young adult in my early thirties, just beginning to awaken to a call to ministry, Dr. Krispin taught me the importance of humility and meekness in faith, while focusing on charging the "gates of Hades" (Matthew 16:18) for the sake of Christ's church—and not at the cost of it. Bill Krispin had an enduring faith that stood taller than any one circumstance, barrier, challenge, temptation, or discouragement.

Bill had a profound love for Jesus that was evident beyond his preaching and pastoring. He had a faith in Jesus that shaped him personally and deeply; you knew it by his prayer life, sure, but especially through his character of godliness. You saw it in his love for Mary, his amazing, godly, beautiful wife. You saw it in his love for his children and his grandchildren. You saw it in the way he knew God's Word and the way he processed it. You saw it in how he would process his discouragements and sorrows; he would recount the way God's Word would shape him during discouraging times. He's like an oak tree—tall, faithful, with deep roots, anchored to the soul the way the prophet Isaiah describes God's people as "oaks of righteousness, a planting of the LORD for the display of his splendor" (Isaiah 61:3), which by the way, Bill often preached on as one of his favorite verses of Scripture. Dr. Krispin taught me not only to be faithful to Jesus and ministry, but what it looks like to be faithful to Jesus and ministry.

Dr. Krispin was the first person outside my own family from whom I sought to validate an internal calling to pastoral ministry and church planting; I will never forget his encouragement to me as I wrestled with the calling. When I considered going to seminary, I followed Bill's guidance to enroll at LAMP instead of the traditional seminary route; it was a relational decision. Bill was also the first person I went to as I prepared to get married. He taught me what it means to be faithful to Jesus, to his church, to my wife—and to tether myself to Jesus for the glory of God through every victory, triumph, and sorrow. Years ago, I endured a tremendous hardship at the church and considered leaving the ministry altogether; if it weren't for the enduring counsel of faithful men like Bill Krispin, Bruce Finn, and Doug Logan, I would've left for good—their experience and counsel brought so much life to me during a very confusing time. Today, as the founding pastor of Metro Church in Philadelphia—with two campuses and marching towards one thousand congregants, I have men like Bill to thank as I enjoy the triumph of ministry through its hardships and brokenness; I learned how to do it by watching Bill do it for decades

In Summary

What can be said of men like Dr. William Krispin? They don't make them like they used to, that's for sure. Bill possessed a grit and stamina that comprised an older, battle-tested generation—a resilient blue-collar faith and work ethic that never rested nor quit. The author of Hebrews writes about Abraham (Hebrews 11:10), who "was looking forward to the city with foundations, whose architect and builder is God." The suburban garden-planting life was never for Bill Krispin, and thankfully, the New Jerusalem is a city. He shaped so many of us with a theology of the city and ministry that has led to the birth of tens, no, hundreds of church plants throughout Philadelphia and all over the country. His love for the city and the poor was real and fruitful.

He taught me as a professor and as only a spiritual father could. As a working professional, I also served as the director of a fairly prominent youth Bible camp in Philadelphia. When I told him that I always attended the second week of the camp in person due to my career, Bill challenged me to email my executives at work to tell them (he said, "Don't ask them, tell them") that I would be taking two-and-a-half weeks off at work each summer going forward. I told him that was unheard of, but he didn't relent; instead, he asked me, "Who gave you this job? Who placed you as director over this camp?" to which I sheepishly replied, "The Lord." Bill softly responded, "The same God who gave you your gifts, gave you this job, and called you to this ministry will provide for you. Do you trust that?" The next morning, I wrote to my corporate leaders and received my time off each year. Only a father or elder brother could ever challenge you like that, and the Lord blessed me with amazing spiritual fathers and brothers, for sure, but Bill was among them the most senior and one of a kind.

I am so grateful for his leadership in the church, his faithful pioneering at the urban ministry training and seminary levels, but most of all, for his fatherly guidance. I will miss his personal stories that hit my ears like American folklore sometimes with the likes of John Henry or Paul Bunyan. That's the kind of person he was—a kind of American folklore character in the church—and yet, so very real and accessible. In many ways, he reflects the beauty of Jesus, doesn't he? On one hand, so kingly and majestic—and yet, simultaneously, riding into Jerusalem on a donkey. The church lacks those kinds of leaders today, but Bill Krispin would refuse the type of platform and pedestal that today's ministers pursue. We will mourn the dearth of great men and leaders in the church like Bill in the near future, but I am deeply grateful for the training, model, and personal relationship I've had for so many years with him. What a wonderful and godly man, role model, and teacher he is. The Lord is honored by your faithfulness and commitment to the city, to the poor, and to someone in need of a spiritual father like me.

TESTIMONIAL: DOUG LOGAN
TRIBUTE TO A REMARKABLE CHURCH LEADER: DR. WILLIAM KRISPIN

I met Dr. Krispin in 2003 as I was serving as Senior Pastor of Calvary Bible Church in the Kensington section of North Philadelphia. Although I pastored in Philadelphia, I still resided across the Tacony Palmyra bridge in South Jersey. I had not attended Bible college or seminary, so I sought to attend a school near my home and church. Several years before pastoring in Philadelphia, I heard many stories about Dr. Krispin and his school. He served as president of the Center for Urban Theological Studies (CUTS) in the Hunting Park Section of Philadelphia. One day, I called CUTS to inquire about attending the school, and to my surprise, I was told that Dr. Krispin no longer worked there. However, the wonderful lady I spoke with asked, "Are you a preacher?" I replied, "Yes." She proceeded to give me his home phone number. I called him that very hour and was invited to his home that evening. I went that evening, and by God's grace, I was adopted and received by Bill, and a beautiful relationship was formed. By God's grace, Bill invited me to attend his new educational endeavor at the time, Barnabas Bible Institute, which met on Thursday evenings at Bethel Temple Church on B Street and Allegany Ave. I attended for nearly a year before Bill shifted to building out what would be called LAMP, which stands for Leadership And Ministry Preparation. One of the first interest meetings about LAMP occurred in my Palmyra, New Jersey home. So much could be said, but . . .

Today, I am an urban pastor, dean of urban ministry, professor, and seminary president with profound gratitude and immense admiration for the man who inspired and impacted me to be who I am, Dr. William Krispin. Bill has been a profound source of inspiration and wisdom in my pastoral journey. His decades of faithful service to the gospel have left an indelible mark on my ministry, shaping how I approach leadership, preaching, and pastoral care.

Learning from Bill is experiencing a legacy of ministerial faithfulness. His enduring commitment to the gospel message, evident in a lifetime of preaching, teaching, and educating pastors, is a testament to God's Word's enduring power. The consistency and steadfastness with which he has pursued his calling inspire me to remain anchored in the unchanging truths of the gospel.

The wealth of biblical insight that flows from Bill's teachings has enriched my understanding of Scripture. Bill's deep dives into the Word reveal a lifetime of study, prayer, and communion with God. As a pastor, he has the rare ability to illuminate the timeless truths of the Bible in ways that resonate with the heart, providing a profound example of how a gospel-centered ministry is rooted in a robust understanding of God's Word.

I want to pay tribute to a remarkable church leader who has left an indelible mark on my life in three pivotal aspects: ministry, marriage, and his visionary commitment to training men.

Ministry: A Life of Pastoral, Missional, and Educational Excellence

Dr. Bill Krispin's (hood name: B-Krisp) dedication to gospel ministry has been a guiding light, illuminating the path to spiritual growth for countless individuals, myself included. Bill's unwavering commitment to preaching the gospel with clarity and conviction has been a source of inspiration. Through your planting churches and pastoral leadership, you have imparted biblical wisdom and demonstrated the transformative power of a life surrendered to Christ. Your passion for urban mission and community engagement with the poor and multi-ethnic communities has created a church environment that radiates warmth, inclusivity, and genuine love for others. Under your leadership, the ministry has flourished, impacting lives in ways that extend far beyond the walls of our church.

Marriage: Life of Love and Commitment

In observing Bill's marriage to his wonderful and lovely wife, Mary, my heart has been deeply touched by the beautiful testament it provides to God's grace. Your relationship with your wife, Mary, exemplifies a Christ-centered union marked by love, sacrifice, and mutual support. The way you both navigate life's challenges with unwavering faith is a powerful testimony to the redemptive and transformative nature of God's love within the covenant of marriage. From sickness to raising and pastoring your children, I have benefited from my family and am blessed with lessons from your marriage in my own three sons. Your ministry of marriage has been a source of encouragement and a living illustration of the profound impact faith can have on the bonds of matrimony.

Mentoring Men: Shaping Leaders for God's Kingdom

Bill's visionary commitment to training men from any race and denominational church tradition has been a cornerstone of his transformative leadership style. His emphasis on mentoring, discipleship, and intentional training programs has empowered men within various churches across diverse cultural contexts to grow as leaders, husbands, and fathers. The impact of Bill's investment in the lives of men reverberates throughout families and communities, creating a ripple effect of positive change, gospel impact, and long-term gospel impact. That impact is reflected in leaders inspired by Bill to start missional endeavors to the Glory of Christ. Ministry endeavors include church-planting networks, book publishing, training organizations, and urban seminaries. I am a direct result of Bill's influence in my launching of Grimke Seminary in 2019.

Countless churches have been planted, and cross-denominational and cross-cultural partnerships have been forged, through Bill's giftedness at connecting and collaborating from a kingdom perspective. Overall, Bill's vision for shaping men into spiritual leaders has undoubtedly contributed to my strength and vitality and all ten churches I have planted across the country. I attribute my spiritual fathering of the sixteen men who call me their father in the faith to Bill's early years as my spiritual father.

Conclusion: Closing Words of Bill's Personal Impact on Me

Dr. William Krispin's leadership has been a beacon of light, guiding many through the complexities of life and ministry. Bill's impact on my spiritual journey, your exemplary marriage, and your visionary commitment to training men have collectively shaped my pastoral, marital, and academic narratives and my individual life. As I express my deepest gratitude, I also look forward to the continued blessing of Bill's impact on me and now through me to my own spiritual sons.

Bill's most significant impact on me flows from his heart for ministry to the city. His love for urban ministry shines as a beacon of hope. He taught me that urban ministry is an extension of the passion of Christ to forgotten places and people. And that Jesus' love transforms neighborhoods, heals wounds, and draws people together in a common pursuit of a better, more Christ-centered urban community. His leadership is a testament to the belief that city limits do not confine the gospel but that the gospel has the power to illuminate even the most intricate corners of urban life.

Bill's ministry stands as a living testimony of God's grace. His journey is marked by pastoral victories and various health challenges, yet through it all, he radiates a joy and peace that can only be attributed to a life surrendered to Christ. In witnessing his walk with God, I am reminded that the grace that saved us is the same grace that sustains us throughout the entirety of our journey in ministry. May your legacy endure, and may God's favor continue to rest upon you and your ministry.

TESTIMONIAL: NES ESPINOSA

Bill, I think we met through Coz or LAMP. I can't seem to remember. Anyway, I know that it was in the early 2000s. I attended LAMP in '05, '07, and '08, because I attended Biblical in 2010. LAMP was a blessing to me and it catapulted me to get accepted at Biblical Theological Seminary. Bill, when I met you there was an innate admiration to be like you in the way you have postured your life to live incarnationally and tell the good hood stories. You are a storyteller of how God worked in ordinary people in the neighborhood and a missiologist in your own right in understanding the city and seeing how we can contextually preach the gospel in the city. Also I admired how you knew many in the ministry of Philly and I would tell myself that I want to be a great kingdom builder like you. I may be a good kingdom worker now, but it's definitely not on my own doing but by your example. The lesson I learned from you, Bill, early on my journey as a young networker, was where you valued people and met with them over a meal or coffee, and the questions you asked were, "How are you, how's your family, and how can I pray for you?" Bill, business was always second or third in the conversation. When I network with people this is my posture as well. We who are in ministry pour out to our congregation but do not ask about our personal lives.

As I was starting in ministry, I remember meeting with you at the diner on Main Street next to the movie theater. At the time, I started to gather youth ministers and youth ministries to do ministry together. And Bill, your phrase that stuck with me and still guides my ministry in many ways today was, and I quote, "What can we do together that we can't do apart?" I sat with you, Bill, at the diner, and you talked about the concept of Ephesians 4:4–6.

> There is one body and one Spirit, just as you were called to one hope when you were called; one Lord, one faith, one baptism; one God and Father of all, who is over all and through all and in all.

While we gathered with youth pastors, we called it ONE based on Ephesians 4:4–6, and the idea was that we can't do things alone but together, and that through Ephesians 4, we are mandated to keep the unity. At the time, I was gathering ten ministries with over 200 youth where we did youth rallies together, youth retreats, youth trainings, and youth leader training. After discussing the verse and the works that the Lord was doing, Bill, you encouraged me to keep going and that I was on the right track. Bill, you have been a mentor and spiritual father in many ways through those words.

In 2009, Coz, Bill, and I started a nonprofit called Common Grace. We consulted with ministries, church plants, and organizations to understand communities, and we provided demographic reports. This was exciting because networking and coming alongside ministries was something the Lord was calling me to. So we set up shop in an attic at the CUTS building. As we met with different organizations, Teen Haven was a ministry we met with to consult, and I ended up working for them. They were looking to hire a director, and I transitioned to keep working with kids. At the time, I was also involved with Timoteo Football, and with Teen Haven, enhanced that work, and Timoteo has benefited greatly from that relationship. But like I said, Bill has continued to push me on and forward to the goal to live incarnationally and to pursue the unity of doing things together and not alone.

Bill has introduced me to many in the city that were outside my circle. He introduced me to the PCA and had meetings with Phil Riken at Tenth Pres. I remember meeting with Liberti churches when they started planting in the city. Bill invited me to attend a monthly gathering with Partners and Harvest, a network of pastors that were sons of the late Pastor Ben Smith from Deliverance Church. We gathered pastors and challenged them to think missionally and to have a holistic approach from church inside to church outside. We wanted the church to think how we can reach those not yet following Jesus and meeting them where they are.

I have said this before, and I want to say it again. Well, I haven't said it in this way, but let me bring in a hood metaphor. As a kid, I used to write on walls with Krylon spray cans, and there were times that we wanted to write up high. (We called it an "up-high."). An up-high was an acrobatic act; I wouldn't have phrased it that way back then, but looking back now, I would. I was the anchor, the bottom guy, then my friend would get on my shoulders, and then another person would get on top of his shoulders. We would go three people high. When everyone was in position and spray paint cans were in hand, we would move slowly along the wall, and the writer would do his thing. I remember yelling, "Don't forget my name!" Everyone involved in the up-high gets credit on the wall. Well, Bill, thank you for being an anchor and letting me stand your shoulders to write on the wall, and I made sure I wrote your name. But you know what, Bill? I'm letting others stand on my shoulders, and it's because you have been an anchor in my life and now I can be an anchor for others.

8

RETIREMENT AND YEARS OF MINISTRY MENTORING AND ADVISING

I stepped down from the leadership of CityNet in 2007. This officially marked the beginning of my retirement. However, the past sixteen years of my "retirement" have been my most effective years of doing ministry. This has been because of the opportunity God has given me to focus on the ministry of intentional mentoring.

I have had the opportunity to invest in the lives of many, many young leaders whom I advise, encourage, and invest in. In my old age, I get to hang out on the corner with a wonderful group of young, insightful, and gifted church leaders. As I let them stand on my shoulders, I have watched them go way beyond anything that I have ever thought or accomplished.

Testimonial: Glen McDowell

Bill Krispin—Kingdom Servant

The Lord has used Bill to shape my life in many ways.

Connector! Bill connects the diverse parts of the body of Christ who otherwise would not be hearing one another. He brings isolated parts of the Christian family together to enrich and enlarge Kingdom impact. I continue to learn from him as I seek to do the same.

Discipler of leaders! Bill raises up pastors, evangelists, and representatives of King Jesus in the marketplace. This has greatly enriched the Church and all spheres of life for Philadelphia and far beyond our city. Other North American cities and huge house church networks in China learned from and adapted Bill's insights for raising up leaders. He trains transformational leaders for transformational ministries.

Way-maker! Bill opened my eyes to the richness of the diverse body of Christ. I learned that the Church in Philadelphia that is doing the most to advance the gospel and God's Kingdom for our city is the African American

Church. I realized how impoverished I was theologically and in my Christian experience by only being exposed to the white evangelical church as a youth and in my training in the Reformed tradition in seminary.

Unifier! He is a model and teacher to me of how to bring brothers and sisters together who come from very different theological streams, yet who have a common love for the Lord Jesus. The work he did in bringing together Pentecostal churches and the Orthodox Presbyterian Church to jointly form and own the Center for Urban Theological Studies (CUTS) was simply miraculous!

Friend! Bill and Mary have come alongside Connie and me over the years as we have struggled with the challenges of raising adopted children with special needs. Going ahead of us in raising their children, their children testify to their godly upbringing, which has given us hope and encouragement.

Bill's friendship with many pastors in Philadelphia over the years has had a profound impact for good on them, their churches, and our city.

Curious! Bill is always learning and communicating about the wonders and beauty of God's work through his people in so many cultures in our city, in China, and across the world.

Leader! Others follow him because he did the hard work of walking in their shoes as a South Philly (and later, Roxborough) pastor, and so had enormous credibility as he trained and loved on the pastors at CUTS and in China.

Brilliant! Bill combines a deep knowledge of Scripture with the research of a sociologist and the statesmanship of a global Church leader to train others to do theology in the urban context.

Visionary! Bill inspired an ongoing gathering of church planting pastors to foster a movement of new churches, reaching the unchurched and dechurched of Greater Philadelphia. In China he inspired a vision for training up house church leaders that would transform their communities.

Husband, father! We know that for Bill, Mary, his children, and his grandchildren are his priority.

I am so grateful to have Bill as my mentor, friend, and teacher. His life impacts others for generations.

Testimonial: Zack Ritvalsky

This testimonial is a labor of love on behalf of a brother, mentor, and friend that I have known for more than twenty years. The exact length of our relationship escapes me. I just know we met while I was a student at Westminster Theological Seminary where I graduated in 2006.

My first time meeting Bill was at the urging of James Smith who was the Pastor of Sweet Union Baptist Church where I now pastor. We initially met at the Manayunk Diner, which at that time was arguably the gateway to Manayunk, where Bill lived and pastored for several years at Pilgrim Church. As I would learn during our conversation, Pilgrim Church was just one of the churches Bill pastored as he grew accustomed to the city and the city grew accustomed to him.

Although I did not know it then, through years of schooling, practical ministry, and life, I now realize Bill was a cultural, anthropological, practical theologian who loved the city of Philadelphia, its people, and the pastors who represented Christ throughout the 134 plus square miles that made up the sprawling metropolis. Bill loved the city because he knew Christ loved the city, and after you met Bill, you could not help but begin a new relationship with the city as he helped you see it through Christ's eyes.

It was this transformative impact that still resonates with me today and that compels me to write about the impact of this wonderful brother in my life. It was Bill who helped me to understand the gospel and biblical justice for the oppressed in the community of West Philadelphia, where I was called to serve in the Carroll Park section of the city. Because of Bill, Sweet Union Baptist Church became active in community organizing and sought to clean abandoned lots in our community, partner with local schools, and turn the church into a place of hope, help, and healing. Quite frankly, we learned how to more deeply love God by loving our neighbor and demonstrating that love by becoming actively involved in making a difference in the spaces and lives of the residents.

Not only did Bill give me a heart for the city, but he also developed my biblical and theological lens, encouraging me to always teach and learn with an open Bible. This personal mantra is what I believe opened the door to so many friendships in his life with pastors who theologically saw the Scriptures through a different lens. But not so different that Bill would divide with them, instead seeking to build a relationship where he became trusted advisor to some, a coach to others, and to everyone, a friend.

As a result of Bill's relationships, he showed me how to be a gatherer and connector. I remember watching him gather and launch a new generation of church planters out of New Life Presbyterian Church under the umbrella of CityNet Ministries. I saw him not only gather but also connect this energetic group to different parts of the city and later to other states through the liberti network of churches. It was also during this season that I learned from Bill the difference between form and function when it comes to the church. He showed me the church's form can change with the generations, but the function remains the same—proclaiming the gospel of Jesus Christ while preparing for the return of the King.

I was also privileged to learn about the challenges of leadership from Bill when he recruited me to be the Executive Director of CityNet Ministries. It was here that I learned leadership is hard, requiring difficult decisions that may not have the crowd's approval but are necessary. During this tenure, while working with Pastor Rick Marshall, we recommended to Bill and he agreed to redefine CityNet by releasing the church planting group into its own entity and moving the pastoral training under new leadership. Bill went along with this suggestion, which was a pivotal point for the ministry God built using Bill, but it was necessary if the church planters were going to have the freedom to grow and to shape the movement as they saw appropriate for their audience.

It was at Bill's invitation that I became an adjunct professor at the Center for Urban Theological Studies (CUTS) and later the Site Director for Lancaster Bible College Center for Urban Theological Studies which now is Lancaster Bible College | Capital Seminary & Graduate School Philadelphia (LBC). This role allowed me to perpetuate the legacy of CUTS. CUTS was started by Bill and others to give first pastors of color and then in general people of color access to orthodox biblical, theological, and practical teaching. People of color were the focus because during the sixties and seventies, they were systematically prohibited from having access to the more elite theological training institutions around the city. CUTS was Bill's way of establishing a level field in Biblical education which, as a result of his involvement, helped redefine pastoral ministry for clergy in and around the city.

The door Bill opened to CUTS and his endorsement to LBC leadership about my ability to be their first Site Director is what has led to my current position with the college as the Vice President of Institutional Alignment. Neither Bill nor I could imagine that more than twenty years ago, God brought us together for such a time as now. It is both my pleasure and reward to thank Bill for the investment of his time, talent, and treasure, enabling me to be all that God intended. I do not doubt that God chose Bill to prepare me for this moment in His redemptive-historical story, and I am grateful He did.

With Fond Affections and Remembrances,
Zachary Ritvalsky
Vice President of Institutional Alignment Lancaster
Bible College | Capital Seminary & Graduate School

Testimonial: Kent Jacobs, Pastor of Epic Church

My name is Kent Jacobs, founding and lead pastor of Epic Church in Philadelphia, Pennsylvania. Bill Krispin is and has been a dear friend, a mentor, and a spiritual father, none of which is deserved by me but all of which is deeply valued.

I heard of Bill long before I met him. He's one of those guys whose reputation precedes him. His work to serve the greater church and pastors in Philadelphia has done more to advance the Kingdom than perhaps any other single person in recent history. I affectionately refer to him as "The Pope of Philadelphia," in reference to the scope of his impact and influence in our region. Though I did not know him in his younger years, I believe I may have benefited most from them. The learnings and wisdom he's shared with me have saved years and, I'm sure, more than a few tears. His investment in me as a leader, and really just as a man and follower of Jesus, is invaluable. I see our relationship as providential, and God has used it to help shape and guide me in so many ways.

I met Bill like so many others have, at a meet-up over lunch or coffee. I would later learn that these "meet-ups" with people were a key to his success. I wondered early on how a single person could know everyone and be so respected. His secret was to routinely meet with people with the intention of asking exactly two questions: "What do you do?" and "How can I pray for you?"

He didn't have an agenda other than to genuinely learn about and serve the other person. He could have easily filled the time talking about himself, which perhaps would have been far more interesting, but he never did. This is Bill. He doesn't grandstand. He doesn't demand recognition or position or applause. He humbly loves and serves. His genuine excitement for the work God is doing through others is a sight to behold. This, like many of his qualities, makes me want to be more like him. He's a cheerleader. He's a coach. He's a friend. All of which is unexpected from the person in the room who could have, on status alone, chosen to be none of those things.

After meeting Bill, it's obvious what a wealth of knowledge and wisdom he is. He knows Philly better than anyone. So, it was a no-brainer for me as a young pastor (early 30's) to ask to meet with him again, and again, and again. To my surprise what started as a few questions about demographics and church planting strategy would lead to my most valued mentoring relationship. Bill spent hours and hours talking with me on just about every topic I could think to ask him about. Pastoring, parenting, finances, leadership, discipleship, theology, politics, social justice—you name it, we probably talked about it. And though I am no expert on any of those things, he never left me feeling dumb for asking a question. He always left me challenged and encouraged. Don't get me wrong; he certainly cared enough to confront. He said hard things, but always in love and always with tact. I've left every encounter with Bill better having had it.

From Bill, I gained a genuine love for the city, with empathy for its challenges and excitement for its potential.

From Bill, I learned perhaps the best discipleship of my children can happen on the car ride to and from school.

From Bill, I learned that prayer is our greatest weapon.

From Bill, I learned to freely share what I've been given with other ministry leaders. We're on the same team.

From Bill, I learned that the real path to impacting our city is through multiplication, not addition. I don't need to build a crowd; I need to build an army.

From Bill, I learned that things are better caught than taught, so it is my responsibility to model the behavior I want to see repeated.

From Bill, I learned that the fastest way to get more money is to stop spending it. (That was a tough one.)

From Bill, I learned to be a student, not a critic.

From Bill, I learned to believe in others more than they believe in themselves.

From Bill, I learned what discipleship looks like and what mentorship takes.

From Bill, I learned what long obedience in the same direction can lead to.

From Bill, I learned that relationships matter and that "loving takes time."

From Bill, I learned to be willing to say the hard thing but always be willing to ask for forgiveness.

From Bill, I learned that the gospel is most powerfully on display when we push past our boundaries to love people unlike ourselves.

From Bill, I learned to prioritize caring for the church that lives in my house—my family.

From Bill, I learned the importance of memorizing scripture, because you can't lose what's written on your heart.

From Bill, I learned that my job is to "teach people to live for Christ 24/7 wherever they happen to be."

From Bill, I caught a burning desire to see "every man, women, and child in Philadelphia have repeated opportunities to see, hear, and be touched by the powerful life-transforming gospel of Jesus Christ." That has helped set me and our churches at Epic on our mission to see "Every Person in the City know Jesus."

I could go on and on listing lesson after lesson I've learned from Bill. My only regret is that I've not been a better student. The good news is that I am not the only student. As evidenced in the compilation of these writings, Bill has multiplied himself through countless others, and together his influence will impact countless more. Bill has embodied the multiplication we see in 2 Timothy 2:2: "...the things you have heard me say in the presence of many witnesses entrust to reliable people who will also be qualified to teach others."

Perhaps the greatest thing I've gained from Bill is the gift of his perspective on this life. Ephesians 2:8–10 reminds us that "it is by grace you have been saved, through faith—and this is not from yourselves, it is the gift of God—not by works, so that no one can boast. For we are his workmanship, created in Christ Jesus to do good works, which God prepared in advance for us to do." I, like Bill, hope to live my life in response to this gift, fully aware that salvation is not of my own doing, and therefore being compelled to empty myself in his service and doing the good works He planned for me long ago.

Bill is a brilliant example of such a life to so many. May my life be an echo of that to others.

A deeply indebted and eternally grateful son,
Kent

Testimonial: Fuji Kim

The first contact with a Krispin was in seventh grade. I infer that Jonathan (Bill's son) and I were good enough friends by how often his face comes into focus from fading memories. Fast forward decades, at a CityNet Meeting, I lingered to ask, "Do you know a family . . . ?"

Providentially, Dr. Krispin (my Korean-ness inhibits using "Bill") answered, "That's my son. Are you Jun Kim? We prayed for you." I must have shared struggles with faith in Jesus that Jonathan asked the Krispin family to pray about. The relationship was off to the races.

CityNet gatherings and Dr. Krispin were divinely fortuitous. In the third year of a church plant in which I played a supportive role, I was more "Martha" than "Mary." While the church grew, I had not. The solution, the reasoning for which I cannot recall, was to find a mentor (alongside my

Dad). Mentors in the Korean church in America that I was a part of were less accessible due to language and cultural differences.

CityNet seemed to be an organic, voluntary network wanting to invest in the next generation of pastors and church planters. The participants were refreshingly more diverse—in generations, backgrounds, and experiences—than in the Korean-American church. The candid fellowship, the humility from the gospel, and the shared vision for increasing His kingdom were rejuvenating, a step in the direction of being mentored. (One fruit of CityNet relationships was participating in the "Living for the King" course by New Life Church in Dresher—something that Dr. Krispin suggested. While by the time of taking the course, I already had a rediscovery of the truth of the gospel, the course addressed my character, which was slow to catch up with the truth.)

In the monthly gatherings, CityNet envisioned God's Kingdom together. Over the years, I have recounted Professor Clair Davis's observation of his experience of the gatherings. In living and doing ministry, one becomes bewildered with the questions "What is God doing in the world? What is the church doing?" Then, we come to a CityNet meeting and hear of what God is doing in the world and what the church is doing in Philadelphia. After a few days of living and doing ministry bewilderment returns. CityNet gatherings were a realization of what Dr. Krispin has often shared, "What ministry can we do together that is far greater than alone?" I needed that ministry and gospel, done together.

Thankfully, Dr. Krispin welcomed mentoring me, one so bewildered about the next steps in ministry life. He shared not only wisdom from faith in Jesus' gospel and ministry but also his failings and weaknesses. With generosity of his time and the fellowship of CityNet, the church planting vision was ignited again. As I needed much training, Dr. Krispin came up with the idea, I believe, of applying to the Redeemer Fellows Program. The program was limited, however, to a cohort of four planting in New York City or internationally. With his recommendation (possibly with Tim Keller being indebted to him), I was allowed to be the fifth wheel. During a Fellows meeting, one of the Redeemer Church Planting Center staff asked for Dr. Krispin's contact. The reason was to ask about his coaching of church planters, a critical ingredient of church planting success or failure. While the Redeemer Church Planting Center could provide training and material resources, good coaches were at a premium.

Dr. Krispin coached me through the steps of church planting with its ups and downs. Sitting in the local diner or the recliner in the Roxborough house, he spoke the truth in love, "Man, you're wanting the perfect plan. There is no perfect plan!" "The vision has to be so big that God has to be in it." "God is not just interested in raising you up but He wants to raise up an army for His Kingdom." (The Krispin-isms are coming back as I write. To share the truths from all the conversations would take too long, especially with my poor recall.) As I am bent toward discipleship, Dr. Krispin stressed Second Timothy 2:2, "What you have heard from me in the presence of many witnesses entrust to faithful men, who will be able to teach others also."

In dealing with issues of church planting and my personal hangups, he saw them as opportunities to stir the pot to see how the Spirit will work. After a season of discussing steps to planting, he instructed, "Your first task is 'Get married.'" My reaction was "How can I keep this advice?!" Looking back, how practical! Even with the best of teams, the church planter carries some burdens alone. After a week of ministry, a planter without a regular, outside voice (like a spouse) could sulk in second-guessing what should have and should not have said, preached, or done. Thankfully, Dr. Krispin prayed at my wedding.

After stepping aside from the church plant, I was more complacent in meeting up with Dr. Krispin. Still, whenever I reached out, he shared time and energy to catch up and mentor. Recently, his counsel contributed to heeding God's call to leave Philadelphia for Northern California. To please my parents as a good, middle child meant staying in Philly for their last chapter of retirement. Dr. Krispin said something to the effect of "There will come a time when parents cannot determine for themselves where they live. Where the children are at, that's where they will go."

As I live in the world and serve Jesus' kingdom, I easily become bewildered. "What is God doing in the world? How is the church going forward? How do I face these tougher chapters of life?" To this day, Dr. Krispin calls as the Spirit prompts (or I check in on him). Along with catching up, I find he is doing the Lord's work despite physical limitations and reduced energy level. I learn of how God has brought him in contact with church networks in the American South and in Asia. Then, my call to ministry in this chapter of life and the vision of Jesus' work and kingdom are clearer, even for a few days. If by Jesus' power I can serve a small fraction of the next generation of God's people (2 Tim. 2:2) that the Krispins served, I would have lived well.

When thinking of the Krispins, Bill and Mary, my heart is full. Their generosity in sharing their lives with me has always humbled me. My words fail. I praise God's "glorious grace, with which he has blessed us in the Beloved" (Ephesians 1:6) through this faithful man.

9

CHRIST AT THE WALL THAT DIVIDES

We live in a world deeply divided on many levels:

- There's the racial divide: black, white, brown, red, mixed race—one asserting that they are better than the other.

- Then there's the economic divide: upper class, middle class, and lower class—no one wants to live in the community of the other.

- The worker divide: the employer/employee divide—one taking advantage of the other for personal gain. Some CEOs make as much as 200 percent or more than the workers.

    What does Scripture have to say to the rich? See James 5.

    Now listen, you rich people, weep and wail because of the misery that is coming on you. Your wealth has rotted, and moths have eaten your clothes. Your gold and silver are corroded. Their corrosion will testify against you and eat your flesh like fire. You have hoarded wealth in the last days. Look! The wages you failed to pay the workers who mowed your fields are crying out against you. The cries of the harvesters have reached the ears of the Lord Almighty. You have lived on earth in luxury and self-indulgence. You have fattened yourselves in the day of slaughter. You have condemned and murdered the innocent one, who was not opposing you. (James 5:1–6)

- The language barrier: when I can't understand you, I don't trust you.

- The ethnic divide: Americans, Mexicans, Puerto Ricans, Russians, Ukrainians, Chinese, Japanese, Koreans, etc, etc.

- The religious divide: Jew, Christian, Muslim, Hindu, Buddhist, etc.

- There's the denominational divide: Baptist, Methodist, Presbyterian, Episcopal, Lutheran, Pentecostal, Catholic—most churches choose to live in the isolation of their affinity group, giving the impression that they are the only true Christians.

First Corinthians 12:12–14 speaks to this.

> Just as a body, though one, has many parts, but all its many parts form one body, so it is with Christ. For we were all baptized by one Spirit so as to form one body—whether Jews or Gentiles, slave or free—and we were all given the one Spirit to drink. Even so the body is not made up of one part but of many.

We are called to the ministry of reconciliation. Not only are we to work to bring reconciliation at the walls of alienation, we are also called to maintain that unity once it is obtained.

> As a prisoner for the Lord, then, I urge you to live a life worthy of the calling you have received. Be completely humble and gentle; be patient, bearing with one another in love. Make every effort to keep the unity of the Spirit through the bond of peace. There is one body and one Spirit, just as you were called to one hope when you were called. (Eph. 4:1–4)

Jew and Gentile Reconciled Through Christ

An important passage defining this is Ephesians 2:11–22, which discusses the Jew-Gentile rift.

The alienation was deep and profound. Even though they lived in the same community there was very little interaction between Jews and Gentiles. Jews didn't want to touch or be touched buy Gentiles. Jew has the covenants of promise and as a result they had access to God in the temple. God from the Jews. That wall was the result of sin. Israel could go into the holy of holies once a year when the high priest entered to make atonement for his own sins and the sins of the people.

But Gentiles could not enter the temple courts. The wall around the entire temple was a wall of alienation between God and the Gentiles but also a wall between Gentiles and Jews. The hostility was deeply rooted in the culture. Ephesians 2:11–12 illustrates this.

> Therefore, remember that formerly you who are Gentiles by birth and called "uncircumcised" by those who call themselves "the circumcision" (which is done in the body by human hands)—remember that at that time you were separate from Christ, excluded from citizenship in Israel and foreigners to the covenants of the promise, without hope and without God in the world.

Gentiles were without hope and without God. But Christ came to change that.

But now in Christ Jesus you who once were far away have been brought near by the blood of Christ. (Eph. 2:13)

Christ comes and makes peace between Jews and Gentiles and between both and God. He does this by making them into one new humanity. Both were sinners and needed a savior.

For he himself is our peace, who has made the two groups one and has destroyed the barrier, the dividing wall of hostility, by setting aside in his flesh the law with its commands and regulations. His purpose was to create in himself one new humanity out of the two, thus making peace, and in one body to reconcile both of them to God through the cross, by which he put to death their hostility. He came and preached peace to you who were far away and peace to those who were near. For through him we both have access to the Father by one Spirit. (2:14–18)

And the gospel brings them together before God. A lasting peace. A new humanity. The result:

Consequently, you are no longer foreigners and strangers, but fellow citizens with God's people and also members of his household, built on the foundation of the apostles and prophets, with Christ Jesus himself as the chief cornerstone. In him the whole building is joined together and rises to become a holy temple in the Lord. And in him you too are being built together to become a dwelling in which God lives by his Spirit. (2:19–22)

We are made into a holy temple with Christ the cornerstone and we are the walls that rise from the foundation to be a holy temple in the Lord; a place where God lives by His Spirit.

And, as Paul tell us, we are given the ministry of reconciliation.

Since, then, we know what it is to fear the Lord, we try to persuade others. What we are is plain to God, and I hope it is also plain to your conscience. We are not trying to commend ourselves to you again, but are giving you an opportunity to take pride in us, so that you can answer those who take pride in what is seen rather than in what is in the heart. If we are "out of our mind," as some say, it is for God; if we are in our right mind, it is for you. For Christ's love compels us, because we are convinced that one died for all, and therefore all died. And he died for all, that those who live should no longer live for themselves but for him who died for them and was raised again.

So from now on we regard no one from a worldly point of view. Though we once regarded Christ in this way, we do so no longer. Therefore, if anyone is in Christ, the new creation has come: The old has gone, the new is here! All this is from God, who reconciled us to himself through Christ and gave us the ministry of reconciliation: that God was reconciling the world to himself in Christ, not counting people's sins against them. And he has committed to us the message of reconciliation. We are therefore Christ's ambassadors, as though God were making his appeal through us. We implore you on Christ's behalf: Be reconciled to God. God made him who had no sin to be sin for us, so that in him we might become the righteousness of God. (2 Cor. 5:11–21)

We are ambassadors for Christ, welcoming those who believe into the family of God. Think of the church as an embassy. We are to welcome the broken and the downtrodden into the family of God. This is true about all the points of brokenness in our fallen world. None of us to be included in this number but through Christ we are. So the walls of the racial divide come down. The walls between nations come down. The walls within families come down. You get the picture. The church is a needy group of sinners who have been brought near to God through the blood of Christ shed on the cross.

When we attend a church we should find a congregation of believers from many groups of alienation but now one in Christ.

When I was the Executive Director of CUTS we were continually called to work for reconciliation between different theological groups. Pentecostals and Baptist sat together in the same classroom. I was often the lone Presbyterian the room. How could we discuss areas of theology where we had such deep differences?

We determined that these discussions were to be with open Bibles. "I believe I got my view from Scripture. Here's what I believe. Show me where I am wrong." Back and for forth we would go, each one defending their view from Scripture. None of us came away from these discussions the same as when we began. We came to understand that we were brothers and sisters in Christ. Reconciliation happened. This motivated and directed the ministry throughout all the years I have served.

10

EXEGETING THE CITY

I learned to exegete the city from my father, who was a life-long student of community change in Chicago.

He taught me to love the city. We never had a car, so we walked to most places. If it was within three miles, we walked. As we would walk, my father would point out things of interest to him: architecture, community changes, churches, etc.

LEARNING FROM MY FATHER

Dad was a postal worker who sorted mail at the main post office in downtown Chicago. He was a sorter before there were zip codes. This meant that he had to know the district post office just by the street address. He could name all the city's streets in order from north to south and east to west.

My father loved to go to a neighborhood on his day off just to see how the community was changing. In his lifetime, he had seen the development of the downtown area of Chicago. He was very good at on-the-street analysis. As I boy, I had no interest in any of this. But when I moved to Philadelphia and began ministry, I found it to be immensely helpful in getting to know the city. So, I have been a student of community change here since I arrived in 1965.

This became increasingly helpful as I was more and more asked by churches about my read on the changes in their communities.

FRIENDSHIP AND COLLABORATION WITH COZ CROSSCOMBE

One very important friendship over the last twenty years has been with my friend and colleague, Coz Crosscombe. I met Coz early in the 2000s and got to know him well after he was badly injured in a motorcycle accident some years later. He was confined to his chair for a number of months. I would stop by, and we would spend a couple of hours talking about calling, ministry, and family. Coz was feeling all alone. Few were visiting him. As things progressed, we talked more and more about the value of higher education. This led Coz to consider enrolling in a graduate program without having an undergraduate degree. This required him to write a portfolio of what he had learned in the context of ministry that was of college credit value. He was admitted to the Bakke Graduate University in Seattle in their MA program. After graduating, he subsequently took up Doctor of Ministry studies at Gordon Conwell Seminary in Boston. He excelled in his studies. He eventually began to teach at CUTS and then joined the faculty of Cairn University full-time as an urban specialist. In 2021, he took a position with the Anglican Church in Sydney, Australia, his home country. In the past two years, he has initiated an undergraduate training program for urban ministry leaders called "The Well."

Over the span of our friendship, Coz and I collaborated more and more. Being asked by churches to analyze and interpret the changes going on in their communities became a strong link between Coz and me in my later years.

It is my observation that most churches address changes in their communities that first occurred ten years earlier, a few will address changes that are currently happening, but almost no churches take steps based on changes that will take place over the next ten years. Coz and I would address this as we worked together doing demographic studies for churches.

We forever asked the question: "What can we do together that we could never do apart?" We taught leaders how to see other churches in their community as partners in the harvest rather than as competitors.

God never meant for us to operate in silos. He tells us in Ephesians 4:11–16 that every believer has the ministry of a deacon, which includes mercy ministry and helping those in need.

Back in 2015, Coz suggested that we write a book about God's call to his church to return to community-based ministry. We entitled the book Place Matters. Among other things, it goes in depth into the topic of churches addressing changes in their communities. This book opened up many opportunities for teaching, speaking, and consulting. If you're interested to know about my philosophy of ministry, you will need to read this book.

Testimonial: Coz Crosscombe

I can't remember the first time I heard Bill Krispin's name, though I think it was probably pretty early on after moving to Philadelphia (1992). The first time I met him was, I think, when he preached at Bethel Temple, probably late 1990s or early 2000s. My first real connection came when someone suggested I talk with him about getting into a seminary to get a degree. I had been rejected by every seminary I had applied to because I did not have an undergraduate degree. All said the same thing: "Come back when you have an undergraduate degree, and we don't care what it is in." After more than ten years in full-time ministry, this seemed beyond futile, so I was willing to pursue any options, and I had heard Bill could be the one to solve this.

We met in the basement of Asaph Studios, next to Bethel Temple in North Philly, where both my wife and I were on staff. This was sometime around 2004, not long before we left Bethel to help with a church rebuild at Wyoming Baptist in Feltonville. I remember asking Bill if he could help me get into one of the seminaries, and he responded that he was just about to launch a new program (LAMP) designed for people like me, and that I should join that. Though it was many years before I would recognize it myself, I am sure Bill immediately picked up on the fact that I had no real interest in going to seminary to learn anything; I just wanted the degree to get access to places I had been denied. This is important to note on a few levels. First and most importantly for this story is how Bill was able to move me into understanding what education really is. Second, it is important because there is a deep element to what it means to be excluded within Christian circles and the way that shapes many of us.

In the LAMP program, I came to make some lifelong friends—such as Doug Logan (who convinced me to hang in when I wanted to quit early on)—and sat under teachers such as Steve Smallman and Ed Gross. One of the remarkable things was that they treated all of us as though what we were already doing really mattered. Years later, I would come to understand this as a crucial element of adult education that Bill had established in CUTS, LAMP, and any other place that his fingerprints were on. Students had a crucial role to play in the learning experience, to each other and also to the person teaching. Bill continued to convince us that we mattered.

In 2006, I had a traumatic motocross accident, resulting in a month in hospital and a year-long recovery to walk and function again. During the early post-hospital days, I felt quite isolated, unable to function in my ministry role and realizing a lot of my relationships were based around what I did for people. One of my strong memories from that time was regular visits from Bill. Here I was, merely a student in his program, yet he visited me more than some whom I had ministered beside for years.

During those visits, Bill would talk of a different way of seeing the Kingdom. As best I can describe it, he changed my entire perspective of church from that of someone down in the trenches who could see only what was directly in front of me, to that of an eagle, flying over the whole area. In practical ways, it went from seeing ministry as only about what our church was doing to seeing a city full of churches all with the same mission of Kingdom work. But there was a problem: the churches were like I had been, unable to see this bigger picture view. I have tried to think of a descriptor, and perhaps it was like a spider's web connecting all these points, except that most of the actual web was missing. Churches weren't connected for the most part, not knowing who was around the corner, let alone in another neighborhood. And so the church was weak, ineffective, strands blowing in the wind.

Bill spoke of what could be, taking me through 1 Corinthians 12 again and again—what if we were actually one body, many parts, working together? A single church could never have all those parts and, as such, could never fulfill its mission in isolation. I was hooked!!! The entire way the Kingdom was supposed to work looked different, and there could be no going back.

I would say I have always been a good critical thinker and had a very good general knowledge and ability to grasp things quickly. It had served me well in moving ten thousand miles to a new city so unlike anything I had ever seen. But this was like going to a whole new level. Bill had turned on my ability to learn entirely new concepts.

Ministry-wise, upon getting back to functioning, I left the local church ministry and came to work for Bill at CityNet. Educationally, I began to see new ways to take in and process information.

I would later learn that I was an experiential learner, and Bill was using my experiences to teach me new things that I could not process from reading books or listening to lectures. From LAMP, he helped me get into Bakke Graduate University to get my Master's degree (without an undergrad!) And then to Gordon Conwell Seminary to get my doctorate. I excelled in my doctoral work, as it was all about what I was doing each day. Again, Bill had been teaching me to integrate my ministry and my learning and my life. Education had moved from being a means to an end to an opportunity to reflect, enhance, and produce. Compared to my peers, I found writing my dissertation easy, as it flowed out of countless conversations with Bill and some of his colleagues. It was never a separate chore or task, but so integrated into all other aspects of what we worked on.

Bill began teaching me ways to start to build the spider's web, to help churches move from a tribal mindset to a Kingdom mindset. I had learned early on about trying to value others in ministry (Gene Wright especially was an early teacher of this), and Bill epitomized these things. Go into other people's space, or as he would usually say, "Hang on their corner"—a very Philly way of doing things. To this day, the value of this alone cannot be overestimated. When you are in a community that others have marginalized or even fear, you don't get many visitors. People either expect you to come to their centre of power or meet in a "safe" space. For Bill, the safest space was where the local people hung out. Entering someone else's space showed respect, care, even love. It showed you valued them and you trusted them. Each culture has a different way of looking at this, and Bill seemed to know each one intimately. I reflected recently how formal meetings with African American pastors were nice, but rarely much came of them. However, attending a service, or sending my students to their services saw immediate changes. That was a place of great value. Very few white people ever entered a Black church. In fact, probably ninety percent of Black pastors I met knew that I must have been taught by Bill, because who else would send a white Australian to visit a Black church?

Entering the space of others was the first thing. He then taught about asking questions, real and genuine questions. Not ones that gave me an opportunity to share my agenda. In fact, he had taught me my agenda was to get to know them, understand what mattered, encourage and validate their work, sacrifice, and love of God, and then let them know they weren't alone. In a city of 1.5 million with 2,500-plus churches, you would think pastors would know they weren't alone. But time and time again, isolation and loneliness were such a major factor.

So many pastors I met accepted my request to meet only because they "owed" Bill. He had shown up for their inaugural service, helped them get access to education, consulted with them on difficult ministry decisions, shared vital resources, counseled them through hard times, and stuck by them. We would later term this "Kingdom Currency," and that became our "trade."

Bill retired from CityNet in 2007, and so my good friend Nes Espinosa and I formed Common Grace, and our first move was to get Bill out of retirement to join us. What if we took the entire aspect of what Bill had taught us about connecting ministries together and made that our focus? What if we spent our days helping ministers see they were not alone, and could in fact have far more impact if they worked together?

We developed demographic tools to help churches understand their communities; we found systems and resources that would help. But most of all we just spent time letting people know they mattered.

This takes me back to 2006, lying in a bed in my loungeroom, unable to walk, feeling isolated, and wondering if not just ministry but life itself was really worth it? It was hard to see a path forward. Bill taught me that my value wasn't in what I did for people (I would have had none then), but in who I was. Jesus didn't call me into His Kingdom because He needed me to work for him, but rather because He wanted me around Him. He loved me for who I was, no matter how broken and flawed—and at that time, completely useless.

It was Bill's presence through that time, entering my space, that was the foundation of transforming how churches moved from tribes to part of a Kingdom. Pastors, and then whole churches, needed to know they mattered.

The lessons continued. Mistakes led to new and deeper lessons. The complexities of communities that had stumped leaders for decades started to unfold.

Near the end of my doctoral work, I started teaching at CUTS, opening up a whole new world of opportunities and then leading to a faculty position at Cairn University. I remember asking Bill before my interview what I should wear. He said to be in my interview what I wanted to be each day at work. So I went in without a tie or jacket and said exactly what I wanted to say. I called out what I thought were their issues and especially their inability to impact those from urban communities. I said I would bring a whole new way of looking at urban communities, one that was built on the churches and pastors they had never heard of, working in places they had never been, and doing things no one outside their community would ever know about. I was "me" in the interview. I left, came home, and told my wife I just blew the interview for my ideal job. I was shocked when they called me back for another interview. Then another and another and another. I was told that most people had two interviews. I think I had five, each one moving up a level. Before each interview, Bill would coach me on being me, not holding back and not fearing anything.

When they finally decided to take the massive risk and hire me, they knew who I really was. I would wear Australian rugby league jerseys to work when others were wearing their ties and jackets. I would take students into the heart of Philly's most "troubled" communities, and we would walk the streets with local Christians. We did things that no other professors seemed to be able to do (get away with??). And I think the results were great across the board. We built an urban centre within the university. I always felt like I was out of my culture and away from "my people" at the university, but I had been sent there from our urban communities, and, as such, I never felt alone or isolated. I felt I had hundreds of churches behind the work.

This was the next level of what Bill was teaching—larger systemic impact. Begin to influence the centers of power. But not by becoming like them or moving to live in them. But rather to work from the margins, the outskirts, to move from the fringe to the centre to show the centre that what was happening in the fringes was not only as important but in many cases even more impacting. (I believe this is what took place in Ninevah as Jonah preached his message. It began in the margins and moved to the centre of power, even outpacing Jonah himself.)

Bill also taught me how students are valuable both as individuals but also for the broader work. I could "visit" dozens of churches by sending students across the city to worship and to learn. They had new eyes to see things we would miss, new ways of relating, and new insights. They helped produce new work and build more strands of the web connecting churches.

At the end of 2020, I moved back to my home country of Australia to take on a new work in Sydney. One of my biggest fears in moving was the distance it would put between Bill and myself. Around Bill, I have always felt a deep sense of security, knowing that my failures will be limited by his guidance and his ability to fix up what I got wrong. I wondered, did I have much chance of making this new project work without Bill? We spent many hours on phone calls across fourteen time zones talking through the complexities of this work, what was possible, what needed to happen for things to work. Bill was integral in shaping a program that has, thus far, been transformative for the Sydney ministry complex.

I have written before that I believe Bill has been the most impacting person on the church of Philadelphia in at least the past fifty years, and his impact on the changes in the approach to ministry in Australia's marginalised communities cannot be underestimated.

I remember in our first class at LAMP, Bill said that seminaries had generally gotten education wrong, beginning with competency and focusing on that. Instead, he said we needed to focus initially on character—that was what would sustain ministry. Competency would come. So I will end in that area of my life. Bill has had a profound ability to help keep people on the right track in their own lives. Almost every conversation would begin with,

"How is Joyce? How are the kids?" (asking about them by name). This wasn't a simple greeting or superficial question, but an accountability. I would share about this great trip I just had, all that I learned, all the positives that we accomplished. Bill would ask in turn "so how did the family do without you?" I would deflect: "I am sure they were all fine". He would come back again and again with questions until I would slow down and reflect on the impact of my "wins" on my family. He would talk through what children need at each age, never telling me what to do, only offering information for me to process. I would talk of a great upcoming opportunity; he would first ask about how each member of the family would be impacted.

I can, praise God, say that I have been kept from moral failure and ministry failure through these interactions. I can also say that both Joyce and each of our four children have known that they always have had a trump card to play if things got out of hand. At any time, they could call on Bill to get me back on track, back in line. This sense of security for the family is, again, hard to describe, yet also profound.

My father was never very involved with my life, and after my parents divorced, I rarely saw him. In so many ways, Bill has filled the role of what I think a father should be. Faithful, present, an encourager, entering with you into hard spaces, picking you up when you fall, gently guiding and teaching, keeping you from making tragic mistakes, walking with you, playing on the same team, and later cheering from the sidelines, available and never giving up on you.

I think the day I can no longer pick up the phone and call Bill will be one of the hardest days of my life.

11

THE MINISTRY IN CHINA (2008–PRESENT)

I'm going to let David Chen tell the story of how we got to China.

Testimonial: David Chen

The first time I met Bill was during my wife Aliece's graduation. Even though we didn't know him, he came over and congratulated her and asked about her ministry with Dr. Jonathan Chao and the ministry in China. His pastoral and loving heart for China and for us left a lasting impression. Years later, when I had an opportunity to start a Reformed Seminary in China, I thought of him and wanted to ask for his wisdom and guidance on this matter. Knowing he's a busy man and we barely had any relationship, I was fully expecting him to ignore my request for a meeting; but he not only said yes but greeted me with open arms at his church. That was and still is the Bill I know: gentle-heart, pastoral, wisdom, knowledgeable, but most of all loving and caring in the grace of Christ our Lord. I went there in fear and trembling because the opportunity seemed an impossible task for me. I was in my early thirties and not the type of a person that would start a seminary! He took great interest in what I had shared with him, spent the day helping me evaluate the opportunity, and, most important of all, encouraged me to boldly accept the ministry for Christ. It is not so much as his words alone that moved me, but his person, his character, his love, and his impression made on me—this is a humble servant-leader of the Lord that Christ has sent to help me to serve Him in China.

That is exactly what I did. For the next decade, he guided and instructed me like a father and spent much of his time helping me strategize and shape the seminary in a way that is both biblical and practical. The seminary not only provided a solid foundation in Reformed theology, but also an institution that graduates students with a loving and pastoral heart of Christ. Words will not do justice to the influence of Bill Krispin in my seminary. He would travel to China, although already in the senior age of his life, but he would still make the time to be in China a few times a year. He would teach at the seminary for week-long intensive courses, 30–40 hours a week, but also spend the rest of the day meeting and talking with students. He encouraged them and guided them in wisdom and love, like what he has shown me. Visiting the churches and ministries of the students, he helped them, encouraged them, and loved them. It is not an exaggeration to say that because of his ministry in China, he has helped tens of thousands of believers there, either directly or indirectly.

I was especially honored that not only was he a great encourager in my ministry of theological education in China, but he also is my great encourager in my life, as well. Even if he's in the States and I'm in China, we would meet regularly through the internet, where he continues to encourage, challenge, and love me in ways that I could not have expected, more than even my own father. Both my wife and I are greatly encouraged and loved by him over the years.

Finally, all this is possible because of Bill's wife, Mary. She is the perfect example of a godly wife and helper. It is evident in our relationship with Bill that Mary is just as much a great, loving encourager. Both to Bill and to our family, Mary has shown us much love and care and humbleness in the Lord. She would always be beside Bill in his numerous trips to China, but not only was she taking care of Bill, but she would minister to us and to the students in her own ways. Many of the students and people she has touched have vivid and fond memories of her as well. When we were together, she would always want to take a picture together, so that she and Bill could pray for us.

It is easy to train a theologian, but it is hard to mold a person in the image of Christ in His fullness. To our family, we can think of no other person that fits this description than the Rev. Dr. Bill Krispin. His wisdom, his love, his care, and his servant-leadership have left and will continue to leave a deep, impactful, lasting impression both on our family and on many churches in China. Our children will always know him as their "Grandpa Bill," and to my wife and I, a true friend in Christ that mimics Christ's servant-leader character, a humble encourager, and a life-time model.

The seminary David speaks of is the Huadao Seminary in Wenzhou, China. We went to China eight times between 2007 and 2017. Each time, we would spend four-to-six weeks, of which, two were always at the seminary. I would always teach a course.

We would also travel to other places to visit graduates of the seminary who were then engaged in ministry. We would also go to a tourist site. Over time we visited Hangzhou, Xian, Shanghai, and Bejing, to see the Forbidden City and the Great Wall of China. We also went to many beautiful places, and we met a multitude of beautiful people.

The Evening School on Yuhuan Island

Jia Yuhua graduated in the first class from Huadao Seminary. She lives on Yuhuan Island, which is just off the coast of Wenzhou with her husband and now two children.

Testimonial: Jia Yuhua
Bill's Help to Yuhuan Church

My name is Jia Yuhua, and my English name is Priscilla. (This name was given by Bill.) It was around April 2010 that I met Bill and Mary. They were invited to teach us "Biblical Theology" in the Master's department of China's theological seminary. It was the first time I saw these two old people. Bill said he had retired. He had always been very grateful to come to China and was able to come to China and explain the Bible to us after he retired. Bill's "Biblical Theology" allowed us to see the coherence of the Bible. He also taught us the method of discovery-based Bible study. I still use this method to prepare sermons and devotions. Although we didn't understand the language, Bill still tried to get close to everyone. He introduced his family to us and showed us that a pastor is so open. During the question time in the evening, he talked about how Christians should marry and love, and he also guided future brothers and sisters on how to view love and marriage from a biblical perspective, which impressed us deeply. In particular, his experience with Mary was a very beautiful testimony to what God was doing in their family. These were not seen in the pastoral families of Chinese house churches at that time. It also made me reflect on why Chinese family pastors put all their efforts into pastoring the church but fail to pastor their own families. This is the opposite of the gospel. Bill's course lasted two weeks, and when they left at the end of the course, it was difficult parting.

I thought they would finish the class like other teachers and there would be no interaction. But when they came for the second time in 2011, I was deeply moved. They could actually call everyone in our class by name. They said that during this year, they took our group photo and prayed for each of us every day. I thought how at that time I didn't even pray for them, but they actually prayed for us by name every day. I burst into tears at that time. I saw the love of Christ in them, and it was melting my cold heart. We were already very familiar with them when they came for the third time, and I felt much closer to them. In the third year, my first batch of master's students were facing graduation, and Bill taught us a course on missionary church planting. At that time, our students in Yuhuan reported that they were opening a training center for part-time workers. They held classes in the evening, referred to as night school, and mainly trained part-time workers in the church who were willing to serve but did not have time to study theology full-time. Bill was very interested in our plan and reminded us that we must carry out this ministry after graduation. He told me that this was a great idea and "God will bless your ministry, so work hard." Bill is very experienced in worker training and has trained countless pastors, elders, and preachers throughout his life.

We went back and told the church leaders about our vision, but the church leaders at that time did not agree with our vision. They had other arrangements for the church and believed that our ministry was not feasible. This shocked me so much that I told Bill that this plan might be aborted. Bill tried his best to comfort me. I asked Bill if he would go to our church to talk to the leaders about this plan. He agreed. I had no choice but to mention it at that time because I thought it was my last hope. I didn't expect Bill to be the same. He was willing to face our church leaders for my small vision. This made me very happy. I was moved. So one Saturday, we took

Bill and Mary to our church. (We were studying in Wenzhou at the time, and Yuhuan was a two-hour drive from Wenzhou, and we needed to take a boat there.) Bill talked to our church leaders about church planting ministry, explained some of their problems, and made the implementability of our vision clear.

We spent that weekend talking about the church. Bill asked me on his way back to the seminary on Sunday afternoon: "What do you think of the effect of this conversation?" I replied: "One of the core leaders of our church did not come because he was in poor health and was hospitalized. He did not hear me." And I was sure there was no effect. Bill said leave everything to God. This is what I was thinking at the time. To be honest, I had no hope. At that time, I made the last effort for this vision, and everything depended on God. I witnessed my miracle. God miraculously changed the leaders' thoughts after talking to Bill. At that time, our church had a prayer mountain, and people from the entire pastoral district would go there. The leader announced on the prayer mountain that our Yuhuan Pastoral District would hold a night school and asked everyone to pray for this ministry. At that time, I fell in front of God and burst into tears. I could only say, "God, you are so great!" I am also very grateful to Bill. God changed the leaders' view of this ministry through Bill's loving service. If it were not for him, this would not have been possible.

So after the four of us graduated, the evening class officially started in May 2013. At that time, we recruited more than twenty students, and they finally graduated in 2017 after four years of study. During this period, Bill also came to Yuhuan and taught students at the night school. Bill was very concerned about the night school and often asked me how it was doing. He always encouraged me and prayed for us when I encountered difficulties. I saw people thousands of miles away caring more than I could ever ask for.

Bill and Mary influenced me. I saw the beauty of Christ in them, and their love, service, and care gave me comfort in that difficult moment. In 2015, I was breathing oxygen to protect my fetus in the hospital. They kept flying over to see me. It was hard for me to speak when I was lying there. Bill said, "You are a good mother." I don't even know if I will be a good mother. I was identified as a real friend. When I had an unexpected miscarriage that month, he was the first to call me to comfort me and read me Psalm 90:15, which says, "Please make us rejoice according to the days and years of our suffering." Psalm 90 :15 was my strength during those very dark days.

Bill always encouraged me during my ministry and never criticized me. My biological father has never been so encouraging to me. I have gotten everything a spiritual father gives from Bill. I would call him when I was confused in my ministry. His suggestions were very pertinent and guided me in the right direction, and their prayers also supported me. I don't know how to express my feelings for them. I think it was a miracle, and my family was far away in the United States. They entered my life so deeply and helped me without expecting anything in return. Who else could do that except in Christ? Every time I hug them it feels like I am hugging Christ. They are my spiritual parents, the greatest gift Jesus Christ has given us.

OTHER CHINA MINISTRY TESTIMONIALS

Cheng Jing also graduated in the first class of the seminary in Wenzhou. She and her husband, Cui Yu, stayed on at the seminary, serving over the next several years in administrative roles. They now are living in Shanghai, serving alongside Dr. Joanny Chang and her team. Cui Yu is working with the counseling team, and Cheng Jing serves in the administration of the seminary. But before moving to Shanghai she served as the administrator of the Wenzhou Seminary that was based in Suzhou.

Testimonial: Cheng Jing

The first time I met Bill was about thirteen years ago. During these years, he and Mary came to our seminary many times, until about 2015. Because Bill was no longer able to take long-distance flights, he had to stop teaching in China. But I know that he is still teaching seminaries of Chinese churches through video recording.

My first impression of Bill was that he was special because although he spoke a different language, had a different skin color, had a different culture, and had a different diet than us, he could always get along with us. Both Bill and Mary always cared about the students. I still remember that they called me by my Chinese name when I came here for the second time. I was very surprised at that time. For a couple of foreigners, after a year, they still called me by my Chinese name when we met. I was really touched at the time. Later I found out that after we came here for the first time, they wrote each of our names on the back of the photos and often looked at our photos and prayed for us, so when they saw us, they were always the first to recognize us. They called us by name and could match names with people. At this time, I saw not only that they were good elders, but also that I was affected by the way they lived their lives. I felt that their care and love for us was very real and not false.

He would eat the same food as everyone else and would even take us out for dinner every time he came. This made us very happy, since we were still poor students in school at the time.

He would play table tennis with us, do activities together, and sing hymns together. (Although we sang in Chinese and he couldn't understand it, he felt that language was not a barrier for us to worship together.) Every time he was excited in class, he would shed tears, being deeply moved by God's grace. After more than ten years, some of the content of the course that year is no longer well-remembered, but the life that Bill shared in class, as well as his fear and love for God, still leave a deep impression on me. Mary would come to China with Bill every time to accompany us and show care for us. She would care about what had happened to us since they were among us last year. She would even remember what happened at some students' homes and the status of their families. Every time Bill taught us a lesson, Mary would sit in the back row very seriously, holding a notebook and taking notes carefully like a student; she would also provide some supplementary information at times. Mary also liked to participate in our activities. I still remember one time Qiao Rui and I invited Mary to do the bunny dance, and she actually agreed. Can you imagine two little girls and an older girl doing the bunny dance together? It was really a lot of fun.

While serving in seminary, I worked for two years after graduation, and only after I got married did I come to the seminary with Lao Cui to serve. There were two things that Bill gave me a lot of encouragement and help, which he probably didn't even notice.

The first thing was that something very urgent happened in the college at that time. A student cut her wrist with a knife and wanted to commit suicide. Although she seemed fine when she told me about it, for someone who had just started serving in the college. For me, I didn't seem to realize the seriousness of this matter until other colleagues learned about it later. The college urgently contacted the student's parents and asked them to take the student back. Regarding this matter, I always felt that I was wrong in some way, and even felt very guilty for a long time, because for this student, she just told me about this matter,

How could it suddenly turn into wanting to get married and take care of someone else? She's back. Some co-workers came to comfort me, and some co-workers came to persuade me, telling me that the college was not wrong in making such a decision. I guess I don't think the decision was wrong either, but I still feel it seemed too sudden for this student. It wasn't until Bill and Mary came to the college again that I shared this matter with them. They also felt that there was no problem in handling this matter. It was just that before contacting the students' parents, if the students could call her themselves. If she is unwilling to fight, the college will tell her family that if she does not fight, the college will take the initiative to call her family. Two steps were added: Let her take the initiative to call her family, explain the seriousness of the matter, and ask her family to pick her up; The college informed her before calling her family. These two steps may have only been said during chatting, but it was liberating for me at the time, because I finally knew what to do better. The helplessness, guilt, and self-blame that had been accumulated for a long time were all released at that time. It can be said that this incident gave me a great release from my heart.

The second thing is that Teacher Bill practices English with me. I never thought that I could directly chat with an American using my broken English, but every time, Bill and Mary would encourage me and say that my English is much better than their Chinese, and they would tell me that they can see that my English is improving. I found that even if some progress seemed so small to me that I couldn't even see it, they were able to spot it for me and told me without any reluctance. Sometimes I just give some simple words, and maybe even the pronunciation of the words is wrong, but Bill can always understand what I mean quickly. Sometimes I need to use the computer to translate what I want to say into English before speaking to him. He always waits patiently for me to finish the translation, and then I read it to him in a poor way. There is no pressure, no need to worry about what you will say or do wrong, no need to worry about looking stupid or foolish. This is very encouraging to me. Every time I made an appointment with Bill to chat, he always readily agreed. I deeply felt that he was willing to take the time to get to know, understand, and accompany me, and Mary would accompany me in almost every chat. I was very moved when I saw two old people on the other side of the world, listening and practicing my broken English with me, sometimes at night and sometimes in the morning. They are using their actions to express that I am worthy, I am valuable, and I am loved.

Sometimes I don't want to continue chatting because I think I'm too stupid. Bill will always come to care for me after a while and ask if we are safe and how we are doing. Moreover, an old man who was born and raised in the United States can understand the lack of confidence, fear, and entanglement of a young person in Chinese culture. He repeatedly told me that I was excellent (although every time, I interpreted it as saying that he was more polite and good at complimenting others, but I know that he did not say this out of false politeness). I never thought that one day a cross-cultural and cross-age American would give me such great affirmation and acceptance. I was really touched. As I write this now, I still can't stop crying from the deep feeling of being loved.

Bill not only cared about me but also cared about other students. I am a person who rarely communicates with people, but because Bill really cares about other classmates, even though they had graduated a long time ago, he still knows more or less everyone's current situation from different channels, and he would like to be with them. You can follow up in different chats. So for a while, because Bill cared about these people, I also had to take the initiative to contact other people; this was a breakthrough for me.

Regarding my further studies, it was also because Bill gave me a lot of encouragement and even persuasion that I finally made the decision to further my studies. I am also very grateful to God for allowing me to choose to further my studies at that time. Now that I think about it, this further study really helped me a lot. Although it exposed a lot of my shortcomings, it also gave me a lot of improvement. After I took over the service in East China, I invited Bill to give a class to the students in East China. Although he was in poor health, he still agreed to record the course first, and then give the class in a one-hour question and answer session. Moreover, his course has given students a lot of help, helping them on how to carry out a ministry—not only the strategies for carrying out the ministry, but also how to view the development of the ministry from the Bible.

I am grateful to God for letting me meet and get to know Teacher Bill. Although his health is getting worse and worse now, and it may even be the time when he slowly goes to God, I am still very grateful and thank God for letting me see him. There are a group of people in the world like Teacher Bill who love God and the people God loves so truly and selflessly. I also hope that I can not only receive it, but also be a channel of grace like them, so that God's grace and love can be seen by more people.

Huang Kai (Jason) and his wife Wan Yen are also of Yuhuan Island. Huang pastored a new church on the island and now serves Huadao Seminary in Suzhou in the role formerly occupied by Cheng Jing. Here is his testimonial.

Testimonial: Huang Kai (Jason)

The scene was our farewell to Bill and Mary at the theological seminary in Wenzhou. In that room, we hugged each other before parting ways. Bill said to me, "You are like my son." And I responded, "You are like my grandfather." Every time I think about it, I feel incredibly embarrassed by my clumsy words. Yes, I guess I am a person with a clumsy tongue, but somehow, I formed an indescribable bond with this "legendary" old man, thanks to God's marvelous arrangement.

For me, getting to know Bill and Mary was a tremendous grace and blessing that God bestowed upon my life. As one of the few students at the seminary who could understand some English, and since Bill would often stay on Yuhuan Island during his trips to China, I had many opportunities to spend time with him and Mary, interacting and communicating. I must admit that during the time I served as their translator, my English skills improved significantly!

However, what Bill brought to my life far exceeded the improvement in my English proficiency. I can no longer recall when our relationship evolved from teacher-student to a "father-son" bond, but it happened just as I experienced it. During a period when I was in a very difficult state, two sentences from Bill deeply moved me: "You are like my son, and I am concerned about you," and "I hope you can be happy." Such care and support were crucial forces in my life. In the past ten years, I have received numerous blessings from Bill—support and guidance in ministry, as well as care and protection in my personal life. Even when I started serving in the church, despite the distance between Bill and me, he remained the one who consistently prayed for me. In him, I truly saw the patience and love of a spiritual elder toward a younger one.

It can be said that Bill has had a tremendous influence on my pastoral work and Christian life. He shaped crucial theological beliefs in my pastoral ministry. But more importantly, he led me in three extremely significant aspects of the Christian life:

Firstly, the awe-inspiring impact of the gospel of Christ. I witnessed this in Bill during his teachings at the seminary. Whenever he spoke of the great sacrifice and resurrection of Christ, his eyes would well up with tears. The two hymns he brought to our seminary, "In Christ Alone" and "The Power of the Cross," still deeply move me, reminding me of the immense salvation of God.

Secondly, the anticipation of "that day." I saw this in Bill, who suffered from severe illness. Whenever he went through the valley of the shadow of death, he always faced it with a calm hope in the glory of Christ. This steadfast hope inspires me to look forward to the day of Christ's return.

Thirdly, the burden for the Chinese Church. I witnessed this in Bill during his battle with a severe heart condition in 2016. Shortly after recovering from a risky heart surgery, he inquired about the state of the church and the seminary through emails, assuring us that he would continue praying for us. Such concern and love deeply touched me. His burden inspires me to press on in the increasingly challenging circumstances of the Chinese Church.

Testimonial: Joanny Chang, Puan Seminary in Shanghai
I first encountered Bill and Mary nearly two decades ago at a Chinese seminarian gathering held at the Jonathan Chao Memorial House in Glenside. During that meeting, Bill recounted how Dr. Chao,

while cutting his hair as a student in the Machen Hall basement at Westminster Theological Seminary in the mid-sixties, would articulate the vision for churches in China. That vision became a reality when a WTS graduate invited him to teach at a seminary in a coastal city in China. Bill and Mary, in true Bill fashion, developed a profound connection with the students, fostering a lasting mentoring relationship that persists to this day.

Our paths crossed again in 2017, this time in Shanghai after Bill's recovery from heart surgery. He was there addressing a group of academic deans and instructors involved in theological education. Not long after, my late husband fell ill. Living nearby, they drove over a couple of times to encourage us amid our misery. It was during this time that I delved into Bill's vision for CUTS and his educational philosophy. With his promise of support as my advisor through uncharted territory, following my husband's passing, I took on the role of academic dean for a theological training program that trains seminary graduates serving their alma mater.

I did not fully appreciate the design and rationale of the structure of theological education until I invited Bill to record a video course on "Urban Mission" for the graduating classes at an underground seminary in 2021. The course is so designed that the students would have to draw on everything they have learned in their M.Div. program to be able to "meet" their urban neighbor. Bill begins the class by coaching students to work together in groups of four to finish the assignments. The students are encouraged to know one another's temperament and gifts, listen to and involve each other, and learn how to reach a consensus. This is his unique way of teaching and applying the doctrine of man.

In addition, Bill adds a segment on understanding and reading the surrounding culture through the lens of Genesis 1 and 2. It is like a mini-course on cultural apologetics, but with a concrete neighbor's face in mind in a global setting. He imprints a picture of Jesus walking in the neighborhood and seeing the neighbors in the street corners on the students' minds. Everything ends with ecclesiology, viewing oneself as truly a part of the body of Christ and with an epistemological bent. That is, unless one can see the log of aloofness in one's own eyes in the body can the church be ready to embrace the neighbor. No wonder we rarely "meet" our neighbors even if they are only yards away! In the end, students have to ground their mission strategy in proper Bible exegesis and theological support. Bill's course is a comprehensive theological curriculum in a nutshell. Wow!

Bill's generous heart for others and desire to uplift every person he encounters from all walks of life remains a profound influence. What I have seen and learned from him will take years to master and implement. Thank you, Bill, for your enduring impact!

Testimonial: Mark Batluck, China Evangelical Seminary in Shanghai—Reflections on Bill Krispin's Influence on Me

On November 22, 2022, I wrote in my journal, "I met with Bill Krispin on Zoom today. He said to me, 'Mark, pray and watch God work—it'll show you that you're not as important as you think you are.'" What a way to begin reflecting on the way God has used Bill in my life. It is 2023 now, and since meeting him at a China Association of Reformed Theological Seminaries curriculum development seminar in 2017, I have been so blessed to know Bill and to learn from the decades of experience that the Lord has given him.

This 2017 seminar of Bill's was very influential in my thinking. Having finished my PhD in 2013 only to spend the following four years learning Mandarin, I was quite "green" in theological education and pedagogy. Bill's "outside-of-the-box" thinking and passion to make disciples showed up in every step of the seminar. Even now, I continue to digest the notes from that seminar and implement them in my teaching.

Since that time, Bill's willingness to meet with me on Zoom and discuss pastoring, church planting, and seminary education as I continue to do ministry in China among other things has been a tremendous blessing. As someone leading a seminary and helping plant a church here in China, Bill's variety of experience in these areas has been an incredible blessing to me. And yet under all of the technical, structural, organizational, or pedagogical advice, Bill always came back to the task of keeping "making disciples" central in it all. He told me once, "Mentoring was never an item on my job description in any seminary or church post. But probably a thousand former students would describe me as a mentor of theirs." And I would certainly be among them.

Another theme that has consistently arisen in conversations with Bill is the importance of remembering that the teacher should "not be looking to give students complete knowledge, but to teach them how to learn." This point may summarize what has been the most transformative pedagogical idea that Bill has imparted to me: the idea that the teacher's job is to "feed students for a lifetime" by teaching them how to learn. Over the past few years, as I have internalized this and started to apply it in the classroom, I have seen the focus turn from me as the teacher and move it to where it should have been all along—on what the Lord is doing in each student's life.

I will end with Bill's encouragement about laboring over the long-haul. He commented on "the importance of serving a long time in one place to see all the 'ripples in the pond.' You need godly patience and a spirit of longsuffering." This is really helpful for those of us in harder circumstances, as is the case here in China. But Bill did not just say this; story after story, he tells of God's faithfulness to him in difficulties as examples of the way God uses these efforts of ours to move the Kingdom forward, ripple after ripple. I did not know Bill before 2017 and apart from that seminar had no other way of meeting him. But I praise the Lord for sovereignly orchestrating that meeting for the glory of Christ in my own life as I ask him to use me to make disciples of all nations. I am honored to be one of the many "ripples" that have emanated from Bill's life of service to the Lord. And I already look forward one day in glory to celebrating how much more God has worked through us all than we ever could have realized. Praise the Lord for you, Bill!

12

MANANTIAL DE VIDA, VALDOSTA, GEORGIA

One of the greatest joys in my years of ministry has been knowing and serving the Manantial de Vida congregation in South Valdosta, Georgia.

Around 2010, Mary and I began going to Valdosta, Georgia for a few weeks each winter to visit to our son Jon and his family. On one of those visits, I was struck by the growing numbers of Hispanics in and around Valdosta. I thought that there must be Hispanic churches serving this population. I began to inquire about this, but the Anglos didn't know anything about Hispanic churches. Finally, my son said that his brother-in-law, Brit McClain, a local undertaker, might know. Well, he didn't know about any churches, but he thought there was a worker in his cemetery who did some preaching. He invited me to meet him on a Thursday at the cemetery, where he would introduce this brother to me.

This proved to be a divine appointment. There I met Pastor Gervasio (Carlos) Ceja, who I learned was pastoring a small church, Manantial de Vida. (*Manatial de vida* means "fountain of life.") We had only a twelve-minute conversation because that was all the time left on his break. In those brief minutes, I learned that he pastored a congregation of fifty people who had bought five acres of land on which to build a building. But they subsequently learned that the land was designated as wetlands so they couldn't build there. He, in turn, learned from me that I was visiting my son and that on that very weekend, I was going with a team into the Valdosta State Penitentiary to conduct a Kairos seminar for some forty inmates. The purpose was to thoroughly teach the gospel that Jesus saves sinners, which we all are. When Carlos heard this, he nearly jumped out of his skin. He said he didn't know how to get access to the prison, which had approximately two hundred Hispanic inmates, from whom he frequently received letters. I invited him to join us the next day.

Our team met at the entrance to the prison, and I took the liberty of introducing Carlos as a part of our team. This was his introduction to prison and began his ongoing involvement in ministry there.

On that team were two Anglo brothers, Jimmie Whatley and Gene Crawford, who took a special interest in getting to know Carlos. They learned about the property dilemma the church faced. Jimmie is a well-linked local business leader who was on the boards of two local banks. He asked Carlos to bring him the papers he received at the time of closing on the property. He discovered that the seller had not disclosed that the lands were wetlands. He then went to that seller and asked him to give the church back its money. This happened. Jimmie said that now we need to find a new property to build a church home.

They found that property. They completely renovated the original building on the lot, all with their own labor. Over the past ten years, they have built a sanctuary building that seats 250 and a fellowship hall that can seat 400. Today, all this property is paid for. Recently, they purchased a three-acre plot of land adjoining the fellowship hall. The congregation has paid off the balance except for a partial loan on the new property.

During this period, the congregation has grown to over 300 strong. It has planted two daughter churches in Adel and Lakeland, GA. And it has planted two more churches in Latin America.

Over the past eight-and-a-half years, I have been privileged to conduct a Friday morning Bible study for the three network pastors and their wives. We have done an overview of redemptive history, a survey of the key sections of the Old Testament, a survey of the four Gospels, and an overview of the epistles of Paul. We are now working our way through the book of Hebrews. Finally, we also have done a thorough survey of the various divisions of Systematic Theology. We often have extensive discussions of key issues facing the church.

I have operated the study on the 2 Timothy 2:2 principle: "And the things you have heard me say in the presence of many witnesses entrust to reliable people who will also be qualified to teach others." They taught what they had learned to twenty-five key leaders, then took it to the entire church using the Discovery Bible Study method by David Watson, a Southern Baptist missiologist. The impact of this on the congregation has been wonderful. Today, they also have a leadership development class for twenty-five congregation members to prepare them to be preachers, evangelists, and church planters.

TESTIMONIAL: ALE CEJA,
FOR THE MINISTRY TEAM AT MANANTIAL DE VIDA

How do God's blessings change your life? This is a question that impacted our personal and ministry lives as we studied the book of Ephesians with Pastor Krispin during our first few months of weekly study over six years ago. We never imagined at that time how meeting and having such a close relationship with Pastor Krispin and his wife Mary would be one of the blessings and gifts from heaven that would mark and change the course not only of our lives but of an entire congregation—and why not say it?—of an entire Hispanic community that lives in South Georgia.

I cannot fail to mention that our walk with Pastor Krispin began in 2008 with a "divine appointment" in a cemetery, where Pastor Carlos worked as a gardener. He arrived motivated to find a Hispanic pastor from the city who could help the federal prison ministry. It was a very quick conversation, no more than five minutes. I don't remember if he told me his name, he just asked me if I was interested in serving in the prison and then gave me instructions to show up the next day at the prison entrance and that a group of people would be waiting for me.

After that meeting, I never heard from that man again. My wife and I always thought, "Who was he, and where he was from?" It was in 2015 at a church celebration when God not only answered these questions but surprised us both—because Pastor Krispin accepted the invitation of a friend to attend said celebration without knowing that he would meet me again. But on this occasion, God had the plan to connect us for his purposes of the Kingdom and create a relationship that has been deepening more and more. And more for studying the Word of God weekly together for six years, not only with my wife and I, but also with two other pastors and their wives.

One of the greatest teachings that Pastor Krispin has given us not only in words, but with his life itself, is how to be a Kingdom person. He has never used the language barrier, his English and our Spanish, nor the distance, since he is in Philadelphia and we are in Georgia, to get in the way of being completely connected (by phone, via Skype, or in person) with our group. We have put aside all our "doctrinal" differences and have learned together "what we can do together that we cannot do apart"—always with the Bible in hand as the focus of our teaching, and not our thoughts. We are a group of people without a high academic level, but that has not been an impediment for him. He has "believed" in each one of us, and in his very practical way of teaching the Word of God, he has given us the opportunity to know, understand, and teach others with humility and simplicity the great theological truths. Of course, he is always joking about "the headaches" and the "Tylenol" we need after each class.

One of his passions is "discipleship," fulfilling the commandment of the Great Commission to go and make disciples, teaching them…—so he has taken great care of transmitting his love and dedication in this ministry area that is so important for spiritual growth of the body of Christ. Without a doubt, the study of the book of Ephesians has made a revolution and reform in the life of each person and family in our congregation. We have testimonies of people who have begun their walk with God as people who have been in the gospel for many years, and the only thing they can say is: "Now I understand that the gospel not only saves but transforms." And this is what has happened; we have seen lives totally transformed and now say "no to sin and yes to obedience to Christ."

The need to train leaders is one of the concerns that Pastor Krispin had in relation to our church, which has grown in an amazing way in recent years.

So he has been given the task of working with us and helping us discover and develop leaders who will help us improve our service and work inside and outside the church. These teachings have changed the point of view of leadership since we have walked based on three principles that Pastor Krispin imparted to us: character, doctrine, and ministry. And this, in turn, has led us to be a church of sound soctrine, where not only do the congregants know the Word, but they try to live under His authority and be a reflection of Christ in our community.

I want to emphasize in large letters that WE LOVE PASTOR KRISPIN and MRS. MARY—not for everything they have done for us, the church, and the Hispanic community that we represent, but for their BIG HEART, their wisdom and experience in serving God and his people. It is countless, but their friendship for us and their love for Christ is invaluable. The blessing that God has given us through having them in our lives has changed our walk with Christ. Their example of love has motivated us as people and also challenges us daily to be better servants for and by our Lord Jesus Christ.

13

THE FAMILY

Mary was the great fringe benefit I received from being an intern at Tenth Presbyterian Church back in 1966 and 1967. I had met her roommate one Saturday at the church. A couple of weeks later, she invited me, along with several others, to her home for dinner after Sunday worship. At that dinner, a conversation was struck up over my ability to tell you who was missing from worship on a given Sunday. You should know that ninety-five percent of church attenders sit in the same seat every Sunday. So, you don't look for who is there but rather for who isn't there. I participated in leading worship, and so I sat on the platform facing the congregation. When asked that day, I listed some key people that were missing, and I made the comment that some women stay home to prepare dinner. Mary, feeling that I was targeting her, blurted out that she hadn't made the dinner, her roommate had. Bingo, gotcha.

Following dinner, the group went for a walk on the Forbidden Drive in the Wissahickon Valley in Fairmount Park. I found myself walking alongside Mary. We struck up a conversation that led to us talking about our families. I saw her love for family and for the Lord. I was drawn to her. That evening, following evening worship, I got the courage to ask her out to go to a concert the following Friday. To my amazement she accepted. We went to a classical organ concert. (Classical organ music is my favorite.) Following the concert, we went out for dessert and coffee. When we were about to order, I realized I only had twenty-five cents in my pocket. Embarrassed, I ordered one pot of tea with two cups. The waitress complied and found it to be hilarious. I knew that I had blown it. She'd never go out with me again. But she did. We met in November 1966, were engaged on March 1, 1967, and were married on September 9th that same year. It has been a wonderful and amazing ride for now fifty-six years of marriage.

God blessed us with five children: Karen (1968), Jonathan (1969), Timothy (1971), Rebecca (1974), and Elizabeth (1976). From them, there are now seventeen grandchildren. Amazingly, all walk with the Lord. There's no greater blessing than that.

Our children attended Christian schools. Only the two boys attended public schools for two years before deciding that they'd rather go to a Christian school. The older three went to PACS for the elementary grades and then went to Philmont Christian Academy for high school. The two youngest went to Spruce Hill Christian School (now City School) for the elementary grades and then to Philmont for high school. All graduated from Geneva College except for Elizabeth who attended Geneva for two years and then finished at Johns Hopkins University in nursing.

Beginning when Karen entered high school, Mary returned to nursing to pay for the kids' education. She did this until Elizabeth graduated from college. Every dollar she earned went to paying for education.

Over the years, we lived in four places prior to our current residence: Norristown (1 year), South Philadelphia (11 years), Germantown (18 years), and Roxborough (19 years). We now live in a condo in Elkins Park (6 years).

To my shame, the kitchens in the first two houses needed remodeling from the beginning. Only in our last month at both homes were we able to get them remodeled. When we moved to Roxborough, Mary insisted that it must have a newer, fully equipped kitchen.

Travels Together

In the early years, our family took many camping trips with our tent trailer (it looked like an Elephant's head) to the Delaware and Maryland shores.

We went to Disney World with Jon and Paige in 1994.

We visited San Francisco and Yosemite National Park in 1994 to spend time with my brother Victor and his wife Emily.

We visited Japan when Karen was serving there as a missionary associate with the Cal Cummings family in Sendai.

During 2008 to 2017, we visited China eight times, spending four-to-six weeks there each time.

We went to Chile in 2012 for two weeks to minister in partnership with Dave and Esther Miller.

We made a special trip to South Dakota when my mother's family, the Jacobsons, held a reunion in 2018. This was a wonderful reminder of times we had spent there with my grandparents when I was young.

For 21 years, our whole family would spend a full week together on North Carolina beach vacations.

We took numerous trips to Chicago to visit family and to Towanda, PA to visit Mary's family.

A special treat was to attend the final regular season game of the Cubs in Chicago in 2018, which was the year the Cubs won the World Series.

Our greatest joy is that all five of our children are walking with the Lord as are their children. The blessing of the gospel has now reached the fifth generation of believers.

Through it all Mary has my faithful support and now caregiver. Yes, Mary is soft-spoken, but also strong-willed. This served her well as she played the major role in the raising of our children and dealing with me. I am so grateful for her love and care.

Testimonial: Karen Bryant (1968)

Everyone has a desire to be seen and known by someone. As a result, do we strive to see and know?

To see and know someone is messy. It is time-consuming. Inconvenient. Take a wrongdoing done by a child. The parent must stop what they are doing, confront the child, and somehow show the child just why the action or words were wrong. Often, that means doling out punishment, which takes more time and excites unpleasant emotions.

My parents were far from perfect in their ability to see know us. However, they were aware of that and grew in their ability over time. My siblings and I were seen and known by them to the point where they would strike at the issue of the heart that affected our relationships with others. I remember once when I got into an argument with one of my brothers my father had us sit down and read Philippians 2:1–11 on our own. He then brought us together and had us share what that passage of Scripture was about, and how it applied to our disagreement. There was no punitive punishment involved. Rather, time and space were offered for the Holy Spirit to be at work in our hearts.

When punishment was given, more times than not there was an uncomfortable conversation about "the heart of the matter." However, the discomfort was in the conviction of the heart. Often that conversation offered an opportunity to repent—admitting guilt, apologizing, and asking for forgiveness. The restoration of the relationships affected was given a chance. I use the plural of relationship because it was not just the relationship with my sibling or parent that was at stake, but also the relationship with my heavenly Father.

I remember as a child being offered by my parents the choice in response to the situation of either receiving punishment OR praying to God, asking for his forgiveness. The state of my heart at those times was to choose the punishment simply because it was the easiest. I would serve my time and go on my merry way. However, that is not what our Lord desires for us. The restoration of the relationship is what is desired. However, that is quite uncomfortable. It takes humility to admit our responsibility for breaking the relationship. It takes vulnerability to ask for forgiveness and wait for the answer to whether our request will be honored. It also grieves us as we realize the cost that enables the possibility of a restored relationship with others, especially with our God.

My parents also understood the importance of being an example to us in this process. Both frequently came to us when they realized they had wronged us and sought forgiveness and restoration. It is the safety of this environment—the consistency of teaching and example—that allowed me to see the loveliness of grace and mercy extended and the healing power that offers.

My parents understood the seriousness of these conversations. It was rare that they shied away from them. I specifically mention moments of confrontation here between a parent and child to drive home the bigger point of being present with people—understanding the need and discerning the gospel opportunity presented. The seeing and knowing.

This is something that I strive to do with my family members (albeit so imperfectly), with my co-workers, with even those that I pass on the street. It is something that I pray my children can know and understand.

"One generation shall commend your works to another, and shall declare your mighty acts." (Psalm 145:4)

Testimonial: Jonathan Krispin (1969)

Family devotions—persistent efforts—built our Christian worldview. Mom often had to herd us as cats towards devotions while dad was teaching classes at CUTS. She was outnumbered! Sometimes passed the Bible around to have us take turns reading when we were being unruly and distracted.

Things that we did in our home as a family, we have continued many of those things with our own families. Music lessons, summer camp (mom and dad serving at French Creek, and sending us to French Creek), family devotions, teaching our kids catechism questions and answers. Worldview conversations at the dinner table.

Dad's interests and how he shared them:

- Going to baseball games as a family.
- Antique cars—Dad loved going to the Hershey car show and swap meet).
- Taking dad to the Amelia Island Concours recently.
- Dad made family breakfast on Sunday mornings and he was always home on weekends.
- Dad came to every sporting event that he could—he loved our cross-country races especially.
- Mom—Gardening and having us help in the garden every year.
- Love of people.
- Chapel starting meeting in our home in South Philly.
- Hosting vacation Bible school in our home in South Philly.
- Walks along Valley Green with the Wilson and Cal Cummings families.
- Dad picking us up and having conversations in the car as he shuttled us around.
- Family car trips to Towanda and Chicago and family vacations; identifying passing cars to keep us distracted.
- Singing in the car on car trips—Becky learned to sing harmonies because of our family singing together and for each other.
- Hosting people in our home after church on Sundays.
- Picking people up and giving rides to church or other places.
- Mom and Dad both working, so we sometimes got locked out of the house. (One time we had to break into the house through the kitchen window when both of them were working, and hadn't gotten home in time to let us in from school.)
- Neighborhood mothers (Mrs. Washington, Mrs. Jordan) who would host us when mom and dad were working.
- "God's Garden Spot"—heard the sermon numerous times.
- Visiting churches around the city and asking about dress codes, length of church service, behavioral expectations, etc.

The life that we lived as a family was an illustration of the investment that mom and dad were making into the community where we lived and the people that we came across. Our home was often a hub in the neighborhood, and our house was a refuge for people, some of whom were hosted for months (Caroline Mapes, for example).

Music was a central activity in our home. Piano was in the dining room and was used often by those of us who took music lessons. We all learned various instruments (guitars, electric guitars, amplifiers, etc.) The instruments and music got larger and louder, but was always supported by our parents.

As a son, I recognize now (more than ever) the ways that my father has poured into me over the course of my life. I have memories of him making it to many/most of my events (sports, plays, choir concerts, etc.) despite his busyness. I have memories of sharing common interests with him as well. He loved music (classical) and indulged in and cultivated a love of music in his kids, even though we gravitated to music that was much different than his own preference.

One particular love that I share with my father is a love of cars. I don't know if this was passed down genetically, but I have loved cars since before I can remember. My mother once told me how she was stymied when I, when I was perhaps three years old, asked her as we passed a parked car, "Why does that Plymouth have Ford hubcaps?" My dad pointed out all of the details that differentiated the different makes of cars from each other, differentiated the different models of cars, and even differentiated the different years of each model. He taught me that I could find the year of manufacture for any American car (at least during the era when I was raised) by looking at the codes that were molded into the tail lights. One of the most vivid memories I have as a child is the day my father took my brother and I with him to the Hershey car show and swap meet. We literally wandered the swap meet for the entire day without walking down the same aisle twice. I saw a car purchased for $25,000 in cash (the most cash I have ever seen in my life to this day). I saw my first Duesenberg in person.

Cars have been an interest that I have shared with my father and has been a bond that we have shared all of my life. Over the last decade, my parents have been able to spend each winter with my family in Georgia, and my dad and I have been able to go to some local swap meets and car shows, and have even been able to go over to the Amelia Island Concours (perhaps the second-most esteemed car show in America, only trailing the Pebble Beach Concours in prestige) on multiple occasions. We have dreamt together of the cars that we would like to drive and own if only we had the means (his all-time favorite car, for the record, is the 1940 Ford Deluxe Coupe. Mine is the 1970 Cadillac Deville convertible). He has called me on many occasions when he has been watching a car auction on television to tell me that he just saw a car that he wanted to buy for me). These are the kinds of things that have made my father one of my best and most enduring friends!

There are several things that stand out to me the most as I have reflected on growing up in the Krispin household. Perhaps the first is that I (Jon) always felt a measure of safety and security, despite growing up in some areas of Philadelphia that many on the outside might have considered to be the opposite. In South Philadelphia, for example, I can remember many times when I was playing on the street and heard adults ask and tell others to clean up their act and language around me because I was "Reverend Christian's son" (yes, many people confused our last name, Krispin, with our faith, Christian—coincidentally, I also remember people referring to my mother as "Mary Christmas" in a similar manner!). I knew from these, and other similar, actions that I was known and that there were many in the community who were actively watching over me. Another example of this protection stems from a bicycle that I had when I was perhaps ten years old or so. This bicycle, which was gifted to our family by one of my father's pastor friends (whose own son had likely outgrown it), was a sparkling, multi-shade, green Huffy five-speed bike, with a banana seat, and the shifter mounted like a stick shift on the crossbar. It was a "hot" bike, and quickly became known throughout the neighborhood. It was well-known enough that it was stolen from me on four different occasions. But each time it was stolen, the community rose to the occasion, sending word out and searching for it in short order. Each time, someone would show up at our door with the bike in hand to return it to my possession, usually within hours. There may have been some danger to be found in our neighborhood, but there were many that were also looking out for our family. God had many angels in place around us!

I have also learned much from my father about how to live a God-led life. As an example of this (and there are many from which I might choose), there was a time when I was a teenager (perhaps about 15 years old) and my father was offered a position in ministry by a large organization that had aspirations to plant many new churches across the country. There was much about the opportunity that appealed to my father, but there were some other aspects about the opportunity that weren't as appealing – for one, taking the position would mean moving our family from Philadelphia to another major U.S. city. My parents engaged us as their children in the conversation and prayer about the position because of the implications for our family. One afternoon, as I was walking alongside my father, I asked him how he could possibly know what the right path for him was—how could he know the Lord's will for his life. He was actively engaged in a ministry that was flourishing and having a kingdom impact on the city of Philadelphia (in his role at CUTS), but here was another opportunity to have a kingdom impact on another order—perhaps across the country. My question to him was this: How can you choose which option is the one that the Lord would have for you, when both options were so clearly Kingdom focused? His answer was that you had to seek the peace of the Holy Spirit.

In Philippians 4: 6–7, Paul writes, "Do not be anxious about anything, but in every situation, by prayer and petition, with thanksgiving, present your requests to God. And the peace of God, which transcends all understanding, will guard your hearts and your minds in Christ Jesus." What my father told me was that, while we might (and should) do our due diligence to weigh the costs and benefits of opportunities that the Lord might place in our paths, these factors alone are not enough for us to make a godly decision. God's economy is not based on the same factors that form the world's economy. Making a decision to serve God means that we need to take these decisions to the Lord and seek his will for us. This involves continually praying and waiting for direction from the Lord. My dad said that being able to understand in which direction the Lord was leading him came from the peace that the Holy Spirit gave him about pursuing one path in contrast with the unrest that he would feel about alternate paths. Even when a worldly cost-benefit analysis might suggest that we should pursue one path, the peace of the Spirit might rest on another path.

I have applied this godly wisdom in numerous decisions in my life, including one similar situation where I was offered a professional opportunity that had many worldly benefits, but, similarly, required a move of my family. While the worldly cost-benefit analysis clearly pointed toward accepting the position, when my wife and I prayed about accepting it, we were not given any peace. We were given peace about staying where we were—the path we ultimately chose. God chose to reveal to us that he was protecting us; about a year and a half later, I learned that the position that I almost accepted was being cut—I would have been out of a job! God doesn't always give such clear information about why He is leading us in a given direction, but I did learn to trust leading that comes from the peace of the Holy Spirit that is given when we continually seek the will of God in our lives.

Another thing that stands out to me from my childhood is that my parents cultivated a strong sense of family on every level with us, and with those in our church family and community. As a family, one of my strongest memories is that we always sat down to dinner as a family. Our conversations were wide-ranging, with questions asked and answered about what had happened with our day, and quite often, spiritual and doctrinal discussions unfolded as we shared the things we had experienced and observed. Given that our family saw our immediate context as our mission field, we frequently discussed how to live as Christians in the world around us. One of the leading strategies was to invite people into our house, and into our family dynamic. In South Philly, when my father was starting Emmanuel Chapel, this included having worship services in our living room (which got completely rearranged every Sunday morning, and put back together every Sunday afternoon), and having vacation Bible school in our house for several summers. The familiarity with our house made it a frequent stopping place for many people, and the number of kids in our family meant that there were always kids from the neighborhood running in and around our house. I don't know if my parents always saw it the same way, but I loved being in the middle of all of the activity.

Closely related to this idea of making our family a central part of our lives are memories of having family devotions after dinner. When I was a teen, my father was heavily involved with CUTS and often had to teach an evening class, leaving my mother to lead the devotions. This was no easy task, as we were quite boisterous as kids. My mother would often interject into our lively conversations words of wisdom along the lines of, "If everyone is talking, then no one is listening!" in her attempts to get us to quiet down. I know that it often frustrated her when she was trying to get us to pause and listen to the reading of the passage-of-focus for our devotions while we were working ourselves up into hysterics, literally laughing so hard that no one even knew why or how the laughing had gotten started. She would resort to having each of us read a portion of the passage in sequence so that we would have to reorient ourselves.

My parents were co-leaders of our household, and worked together to pour an understanding of who God is and what it meant to live our lives for Him. Observing the way that they walked out their salvation with conviction and integrity was compelling to me, even as a child. One of the results of this is that it never occurred to me to rebel against them. I knew that they loved me, and that they were doing their best to encourage me in all of the things that I did (part of their modeling of the self-sacrificial love of Christ), so, even when it wasn't what I wanted, I was willing to submit to the decisions that they made on my behalf—like saying "no" when I asked about going to a party or gathering of friends, for example.

These things deeply impacted the way that I have tried to lead my family as my wife and I raised our kids. We started by teaching the children's catechism to them when they were quite young, and carried it forward with family devotions (although, I don't think that we were quite as consistent as I remember from my own upbringing!). With four kids of our own, we often faced the same struggle to reign in our kids that my mother (and father, on occasion) faced! The nightly conversations at the dinner table were also a tradition, as we helped our kids work through what it meant to live as Christians in their respective circle of friends. I don't think that the power of a God-centered family can be overestimated in its ability to be a light in the world.

Our family often sang together, and one of the songs we have sung together most often is my father's favorite hymn, a hymn that was his mother's favorite hymn, and reflects this focus on family, particularly the family of God, but reflected in the refuge that our family was for me. The hymn is "Children of the Heavenly Father." Here are the words:

1. Children of the heav'nly Father,
   safely in His bosom gather;
   nestling bird nor star in heaven
   such a refuge e'er was given.

2. God His own doth tend and nourish;
   in His holy courts they flourish.
   From all evil things He spares them;
   in His mighty arms He bears them.

3. Neither life nor death shall ever
   from the Lord His children sever;
   unto them His grace He showeth,
   and their sorrows all He knoweth.

4. Praise the Lord in joyful numbers:
   Your Protector never slumbers;
   At the will of your Defender
   Every foeman must surrender.

5. Tho' He giveth or He taketh,
   God His children ne'er forsaketh;
   His the loving purpose solely
   to preserve them pure and holy.

Testimonial: Timothy Krispin (1971)

Just inside the front door of our small rowhouse in South Philadelphia stood my parents' Ivers and Pond upright piano. Many days, my mother would sit and play tunes from a hymnal, just as her mother had done in her childhood home. And, just as her mother had done, my mom gave piano lessons to her own children—with varying degrees of success.

Her playing and teaching were both in praise of the King of Kings, but also a call to her household to join her in skillful praise. That call is part of a legacy that I've seen span four generations—from my grandmother through to my own children. It's a testament to how our Heavenly Father works through ordinary acts of obedience to extend His kingdom and equip His children for His praise.

For me, personally, the sounds of the piano were more than a means of worship. In a small but profound way, making music added beauty to our household that contrasted the continuous concrete and asphalt at our feet, the brick and cinder block used to construct the houses and businesses on our street, and the vacant lot and bars that bracketed our block. From the harmonious sounds that we created, to the beauty of the inner workings of the piano itself, music demonstrated the creativity and graciousness of God, Himself. It was a reminder that we—His children—are called to use all of our creative powers to bring forth a beautiful testimony to a world that seems to be full of death and chaos.

Music also had the power to connect our household to others. The church my father planted and pastored met in our living room for a few years. Before I could read, I knew the words to a dozen old hymns that I heard the saints sing together on Sundays. Before I was done with kindergarten, I was able to sing the harmonies I had heard the better voices sing, as well as the ones my older sister taught me. When I started playing guitar at twelve years old, it was a family friend who helped me pick out my first instrument and then introduced me to his favorite players' recordings. At its best, making music was a group affair—a family affair. We were better together.

A legacy, a source of beauty, a means of fellowship. In addition, the music of our house was full of a great and unfailing hope. That hope is that the Lord will see us through this life and will call us home to be with Him. He is the Great King above all kings. He is Creator and Lord of all. His faithfulness will not fail, and His great faithfulness is the theme of our song in this life as well as in the next. The older I get, the sweeter that promise becomes. I look forward to that beautiful day when the voices of all the saints will be heard joining as one in that beautiful, eternal song. The joy of sharing that hope with mom and dad is such a joy and delight to me.

Psalm 100 (ESV)

Make a joyful noise to the Lord, all the earth!
Serve the Lord with gladness!
Come into his presence with singing!

Know that the Lord, he is God!
It is he who made us, and we are his;
we are his people, and the sheep of his pasture.

Enter his gates with thanksgiving,
and his courts with praise!
Give thanks to him; bless his name!

For the Lord is good;
his steadfast love endures forever,
and his faithfulness to all generations.

TESTIMONIAL: REBECCA OURSLER (1974)

My father has always said that chaos comes with the third child so as the fourth of five, it is safe to say that I grew up in the chaos of the Krispin household. As Krispin kids, we have many shared experiences like splitting the extra hot dogs five ways, calling out numbers returning from long road trips to claim our turns in the one bathroom, announcing "locked seat" if you had to leave your spot on the couch while watching a family show and waking up on Sunday mornings to my father yelling up the stairs "breakfast in the rear of the train".I never really stopped to think about why I can identify a car's make and model with a quick glance in my rear view mirror or why I know the first and last names of most of the members of the 1980 Phillies World Series Champion Team when I was only 5 and half when they won but both of those are because I grew up as a Krispin.

With three kids of my own, I try to organize the chaos and it often gets away from me. But the thing I learned growing up is that there are messes worth making. And instead of trying to hide our chaos, my parents often invited others into it. People came first. If we had room in our car and could give someone a ride,it was a no brainer. If it snowed and the walk needed to be shoveled, we shoveled all of the walks of the elderly on the block. If someone didn't have a place to go for a holiday meal, they were welcomed to our table. And along with the everyday stuff, I don't think my father ever said no when asked to counsel a struggling church where the presbytery needed to get involved. He carried that weight time and time again because the Church is a messy place full of sinners who need Christ. God doesn't call us to be perfect in our chaos but he does call us to love one another. "They will know that you are my disciples because you love one another."

My parents encouraged us to develop our gifts and abilities and pursuits as individuals. I think they understood the pitfalls of making a kid pursue something because of pressures of outside expectations. We were expected to fulfill the commitments that we made and work to the best of our abilities, but we weren't expected to be perfect. My parents were there for us consistently to encourage us, coming to many sporting events and school concerts. Because they showed up in the little moments, it meant more when my dad would take me out to lunch to talk about the bigger decisions that loom from time to time. He would take the time to understand what I was thinking in those decisions and offer guidance. He was always careful to guide and support and not impose his choice on me. I remember taking him car shopping with me and test driving several cars. We talked about the strengths and weaknesses of each one but he never said which one he preferred. He taught me how to make decisions on my own.

My mom has always been a nurturer. She carried a huge burden over the years managing all of the moving pieces in our home and we never heard her complain (except when there were way too many glasses in the sink at the end of a day). Even as I moved out on my own, my mom would often bring a casserole that she "accidently" made an extra of and wash the dishes in my sink.

Because my parents welcomed others into our chaos, there are many more that consider my parents as a surrogate mom and dad/grandma and grandpa. They have genuinely loved this extended family as part of their own. You see many of these faces on their electronic picture frame in their home. They have desired that this family love Christ and make Christ known. It is a family that extends around the world. I have seen God's faithfulness to our family through generations and I know he will continue to be faithful to this extended family. To God be the glory.

Testimonial: Elizabeth Huhnken (1976)

Our household was always bustling. Particularly Sundays. Sunday mornings would come and I (Elizabeth) knew it was my business to get ready for church. Just as this was the business of every member of my household. Sunday mornings meant that you would enjoy a pancake and egg breakfast cooked by Dad and then out the door to church we would go. Piling into our family station wagon. And later as my older siblings started to drive we would often take at least two cars to church. There were many Sundays we would give a ride to someone in our church family who didn't have their own car. So we would make room and get to catch up on life's happenings with those friends on the way to and from church. We learned from those Sunday drives with two specific women in particular that God cared about the smallest details and provided for others in so many ways as they talked about how God had met them and cared for them in the past week.

While Dad made Sunday breakfast, my mom was getting Sunday dinner ready so that we could sit down as a family to eat when we got home from church. There was always plenty of food as we either were already expecting guests or we were ready to invite last-minute guests over. Sunday afternoon dinner often seemed to happen in slow motion as we would take time to enjoy food and conversation with whoever came. We brought out the folding table to add on to the end of our dining room table as the dining room table was where we would eat when we had guests. And we pulled the piano bench over from the piano to the table to make room for everyone. Being the youngest I often had the honor of sitting on that bench. After dinner, the conversation would move on to the living room for some and the kitchen for others who helped us clean up. More talking happened while someone washed and someone dried and someone else put away dishes. More laughter and stories would continue as we'd often drive to Valley Green to go for a walk with those same friends.

Those Sunday conversations opened my eyes to see and my ears to hear about other's lives beyond my own. Learning to ask questions that allowed people to tell their stories. And to hear of others' daily lives, of people who lived near and others who had lived far away. To learn that the world was bigger than what was in front of me. These conversations showed me that God cared about people far different than me. God was gracious to provide these opportunities to meet so many different people and also to get to learn from my parents how to care about people. I got to watch as my parents built friendships with many different people. And built friendships where they could encourage others and be encouraged by others in the truth and love of Jesus.

This theme of investing in people in getting to know them went beyond Sundays as well. I think of my own personal relationship with my parents. As the youngest of five I spent a lot of time in the car with my dad, especially as he drove to pick my mom up from work or when he drove to pick my siblings up from various extracurricular events. My dad took the time to get to know me and asked me questions about what I was thinking about—including my faith and about the future. I remember from a young age my parents encouraging me to make decisions about my future while seeking God for guidance. And I knew that just like my parents and our family friends knew God was with them every step of the way caring for them and guiding them—God was with me guiding me, as well. And just like I know God is guiding my own family and church family, too.

Here is a hymn that we sang in our church growing up and was sung at my own church this past week that reminds me of what we learned in these many conversations that happened because my parents cared to love and get to know so many different people.

His Eye is On the Sparrow

Why should I feel discouraged,
Why should the shadows come,
Why should my heart be lonely,
And long for heaven and home,
When Jesus is my portion?
My constant friend is He:
His eye is on the sparrow,
and I know He watches me;
His eye is on the sparrow,
And I know He watches me.

I sing because I'm happy,
I sing because I'm free,
For His eye is on the sparrow,
And I know He watches me.

"Let not your heart be troubled,"
His tender word I hear,
And resting on His goodness,
I lose my doubts and fears;
Though by the path He leadeth,
But one step I may see;
His eye is on the sparrow,
And I know He watches me;
His eye is on the sparrow,
And I know He watches me.

Whenever I am tempted,
Whenever clouds arise;
When songs give place to sighing,
When hope within me dies,
I draw the closer to Him,
From care he sets me free.
His eye is on the sparrow,
And I know He watches me.
His eye is on the sparrow,
And I know he watches me.

14

How God Used Illnesses to Keep Me Focused on Christ

God used illness to remind me that my salvation and ministry were not of myself (Ephesians 2:8–10), but entirely the work of God's grace.

Rheumatic Fever (1949–1950)

I had rheumatic fever at age five, which resulted in a heart murmur. I missed half of my kindergarten year as well as the first half of first grade. I was not kept back because my mother home-schooled me and I was at grade when I returned to school. At the same time as this, my younger sister, then one year old, had polio. My mother would exercise her arms and legs four times each day. My mother's loving care spoke loudly of her Christian character.

Mono (1979)

I am so thankful for a phone call I received back in 1979 from a dear older fellow pastor who would show incredible interest and care for me. One morning he called me to tell me that he had prayed for me that morning. I thought that it was a little strange, as I knew that he prayed for me regularly. But then he said that he had called me not to tell me that he had prayed for me, but rather, what he had prayed for me. He said that he had prayed that God would teach me to care for the church that lived in my own home, my family. I had five children that were 11, 10, 9, 5, and 3 at the time. His challenge stayed in my heart in the succeeding weeks. I pondered what his words meant.

Several weeks later, I had returned from a Saturday board meeting of CUTS. I laid down on the couch and fell asleep. I did not get up for sixteen weeks. I had no energy to get up. I learned that I had a severe case of mononucleosis. I ran a high fever for many weeks. As I lay in bed, I became a fly on the wall of my own house. My family's life continued as usual around me. I heard what I had been ignoring for far too many years. I had no idea what I had been missing. The phone seemed to ring constantly, and the doorbell rang often, not to mention the swirling life of five young children. This led me to make significant changes in my life that resulted in my investing myself more in the lives of my wife and children. Today, I have the joy of seeing my children and their children walking in the way of the Lord. For that word of encouragement, I am eternally grateful. I am so thankful for the faithful labors of Dave Garnett and Michele Black, who kept the program going at CUTS. This was only our second year of operation.

Stroke (1999)

While vacationing on a beach in North Carolina with my family, I had a stroke, landing me in a hospital there in the midst of a hurricane. This was not your typical stroke. Normally, there are two types of strokes: a vessel blockage or a bleed in the brain. I had neither. The vessel to my brain had simply constricted. I was initially paralyzed on my left side for three days, but this ended when I was treated with relaxing meds. However, I was left with extreme fatigue. I struggled with this for six months. I had always been a multi-tasker, but now I could barely do a single task. My brain needed to be rewired.

One day during this time, Pastor John Yenchko, then of New Life Church in Glenside, paid me a pastoral visit. I told him I felt worthless, that my life was useless, because I could do nothing. He immediately told me that my life wasn't useless—that I sat in a very strategic place. I had all day to pray; I now had the opportunity to pray for the church in Philadelphia. He suggested I take a map of Philadelphia and pray for ministries throughout the city, neighborhood by neighborhood. I did this, and as I did, I was amazed by what was happening all over the city. And I had no hand in any of it!

I discovered several things from this. First, God does answer prayers. I learned to pray—and I learned that such prayers are a way of accessing the power of God. Second, God's answer did not use me in any other way than as a pray-er. This lesson has stayed with me.

Hip Replacement (2013)

At age seventy my body began to fall apart. I went to an orthopedic surgeon, who told me the pain I was having was my knee. I received cortisone shots for a period, but these were only temporary fixes. The pain could be excruciating at times. I finally concluded that I needed surgery, but I determined to go to the Rothman Institute at Jefferson Hospital. Dr. Bill Hosack was the surgeon. Using x-rays, he saw that it was not my knee, but rather my hip. I asked why I was experiencing so much pain in my knee. He said: "Remember that the hip bone is connected to the leg is connected to the knee and so on down the leg." He was right—after surgery I had no pain in my knee or my hip. It took six months to fully recover. Amazing!

Knee Replacement (2015)

Around a year later, I began to have major pain in the other knee. I again went to Dr. Hosack for surgery. It also took six months to recover.

Heart Failure (2015–present)

The final illness was heart failure. The first occurrence was later in 2015, resulting in triple bypass surgery. The surgery didn't go as planned. The first night, I had to be taken back to surgery to repair some bleeding in the heart. Consequently, I was in the intensive-care unit for a full week and was fully intubated. I finally regained consciousness and, after another three weeks, was discharged to in-patient rehab at Good Shepherd in Center City, where I spent another five weeks before finally returning home. The recovery was long and hard. Subsequently, I have had several other occurrences of heart failure. Most recently, in the fall of 2023, I had congestive heart failure and spent four days at Penn Presbyterian. I also had pneumonia. Upon returning home I went on hospice care and on oxygen. In August, I learned that my heart had continued to weaken over the past year in four different areas. The heart failure only accelerated the decline.

How I'm Handling All This Spiritually

I am often asked how I'm handling this continual flood of illnesses.

First, I thank God every day that He grants me another day. It's an undeserved gift from God.

Second, while in the hospital for heart surgery, I had lots of time to reflect on my mortality. I then reflected on what I really believed. I was drawn to Romans 6, where Paul tells us that we died with Christ and rose again when He arose. My death was already behind me. Death is just the door from this life into eternal life. No time lapse.

Third, I was reminded of First Corinthians 15—that death is swallowed up in victory.

So I have complete peace. I am always filled with praise when I hear James Ward's "Death is Ended." This is a marvelous exegesis of First Corinthians 15 in song. He concludes by saying over and over again: "Victory!"

So I'm at complete peace, and I accept my assignment from God. Please rejoice with me.

Postscript

The most productive years of my life have been those after I retired. I've mentored more people and built a multitude of new connections since then, particularly in China and in Valdosta, GA with Manantial DeVida.

I learned that my ministry was more effective than I ever thought, particularly as the pastor of Pilgrim Church in Manayunk and with CityNet. My tenure was short at Pilgrim because of my stroke in 1999. Interestingly, though I was feeling that I was failure as the pastor because of my low energy, nobody in the church ever said that I was not giving my all and my best.

My disappointment with my time as the Executive Director of CityNet came mostly from the challenges that immediately arose from the supporting New Life Network. I felt totally disconnected from the network, especially after John Yenchko moved to Long Island. But I now see that many of the ministries that CityNet initiated had very significant impact in the broader church community. (See Bruce Finn's and Doug Logan's testimonials.)

I promoted the Scriptures' call to the unity of the church over the course of my ministry. This shaped much of my work at CUTS and CityNet. I learned this very early in my ministry when I became a part of the Pastor's prayer group in West Philadelphia.

I saw the love that God had for the city because of its people. I often preached a sermon on Psalm 148, "The City, the Garden Spot in God's Creation." I learned to see that beauty in the life of God's people in the city.

I did not give too much attention early on to mentoring and developing leaders. Mentoring was not in my job description, but as time progressed, I always made time for these relationships. Dr. John Perkins, in 1975, spent a week teaching for us in Philly. As he and I moved about the city that week, he saw my connections to many churches and leaders. He said that the church needs people who hang out on the corner, directing traffic and connecting people together for ministry. His counsel at that time influenced my decision to leave the pastorate at Emmanuel Chapel and to assume the full-time role of developing CUTS.

Throughout my life, I always struggled with writing. I thought that I could never write a book. As I was writing this, I was surprised by the amount of written material I had on my computer. I forgot that in 1994, I had compiled a book on discipleship, which came from a sixteen-sermon series I preached at Emmanuel Chapel. Lisa Tobin, a sister in the church, took the recordings and transcribed them. I then took them and arranged my thoughts on paper. Photocopies of this were used in classes at CUTS for some twenty years. Currently, I'm reworking it for publication. My thinking about discipleship has developed significantly since then.

Appendix A
CUTS Constitution, Article II—Preamble
(Adopted October 1979)

We confess with shame the sinful division within the body of Christ that has been caused by racial and cultural prejudice. Early in our nation's history, the church was divided into alienated units when white Christians failed to receive their Black brothers and sisters into the fullness of fellowship and ministry in the church. This sinful schism in the United States was the result of the white man's stealing the Black man from his African home and cruelly enslaving him to the destruction of his family and personal integrity. This alienation continues today and manifests itself in our failure both to submit and to minister to one another. Alienation can also be seen in other ethnic and poor church communities in the United States. The unity of the body of Christ necessitates that these churches today actively seek ways together of meeting each other's needs.

Furthermore, the continuing racism, classism, individual sin, and corporate structural evils in our society have had a devastating effect on major portions of the urban population. Hardest hit has been the Black and ethnic poor. Thus, the opportunities for higher education have either been altogether denied to them or have been effectively nullified by inadequate educational preparation and provision. The urban church that has arisen in this situation has developed a non-formal model of ministerial training, in contrast to the pattern of formal academic preparation in colleges and graduate schools of theology.

The non-formal model of training characteristic of urban ethnic churches has strengths that formal academic education lacks. The strengths of this apprenticeship model include the development of maturity, the practical demonstration and improvement of ministerial gifts, and the establishment of fellowship between the leader and the church served. Further, the oral communication that preserved the gospel in the Black church nurtured genuine depth of understanding.

If the cycle of racism, classism, and non-recognition of the competence of these church leaders is to be broken, a fair assessment of true competence must be developed. Also, credentialed theological training must be made attainable for these church leaders within the apprenticeship model of their churches as well as within Christian educational institutions.

Further, churches among Black and ethnic poor and the rest of Christ's church must begin to heal the racial and cultural divisions by seeking to strengthen one another and to open avenues for communication and sharing of resources.

These needs find their meaning and urgency in the unity of Christ's church and her calling to preach good news to the poor, proclaim freedom for the prisoners, recovery of sight for the blind, liberation for the oppressed, and to announce that the time has come when the Lord will save His people. The full ministry of the church in word and deed must be a leaven in society and a light to the world. Thus, it is to these needs that the purpose of the Center for Urban Theological Studies is addressed.

Appendix B
CUTS Constitution, Article VI—
Foundations for Doing Theology in Ministry

Section One. We confess that mankind was created in the image of God and fell into sin in Adam. Man has continued in this sin by attempting to substitute himself for God as Lord of life. In this rebellion, he corrupts every aspect of his corporate and individual life and so justly incurs the wrath and curse of God. In his sin man is not only alienated from God but is also alienated from his fellow man individually and corporately. As a result, national, cultural, economic and racial strife characterizes today's broken order.

Section Two. We confess that it is the Triune God, Himself, the sovereign Creator and Lord of the universe, who, by grace alone, is redeeming in the Lord Jesus Christ a people for Himself, zealous for good works. Jesus, God the Son, yet fully man, has fully satisfied divine justice by His perfect obedience and sacrifice of Himself to God. He has reconciled His church in one body through the cross.

Section Three. We confess that Christ saves and rules His people in the power of the Holy Spirit through Whom He calls them into His body, the church, and enables them to live in thankful obedience. They thereby seek to glorify God in every aspect of life upon earth, turning away from what God's Word forbids and seeking to fulfill, as members of Christ's church on earth, the work, worship, and witness for the Kingdom of God which God's Word requires.

Section Four. We confess these truths of the Christian faith to be taught in the Scriptures of the Old and New Testaments which are the Word of the Triune God, the only living and infallible authority by which God directs the faith and life of His people as He leads them into the fullness of the blessings of His Kingdom in Christ.

Section Five. We confess that God Himself dwells with His people, the church, in faithfulness to His covenant promises and that He has commissioned His church to make disciples of all nations. Christ's church is one body with many members from every culture, nation, race and language, called to speak the truth to one another in love and to share ministry gifts, until we've all attained unity in the faith and in the knowledge of the Son of God and become mature, attaining the full measure of perfection found only in Christ.

Section Six. The Holy Spirit has taught these truths of Scripture that we confess to His worldwide church through the ages. Therefore, we treasure the grasp of these Biblical truths conveyed in the oral confessional tradition of the Black and other ethnic poor churches, as well as in the written summary statements of the classical Reformed creeds and other written confessions of the church of Jesus Christ. These oral and written confessions were formulated by Christ's church to answer the needs of the church and the challenge facing her in the travail of her pilgrimage in the way of the Lord.

Section Seven. We acknowledge that we have been divided too long by cultural and racial walls of partition, thereby failing to minister to one another in Christ. Therefore, we wish to bring together these two differing confessional traditions on the foundation of the Scriptures and the finished work of Christ, in a common, on-going process of relating God's Word confessionally to the present issues and needs facing the urban church. We willingly submit to one another, in the Lord, always teaching, reproving, correcting and encouraging one another as we seek together to develop ways of bringing to fulfillment the whole counsel of God in our life and ministry. For this reason, we desire to establish our work with the confession of these Biblical truths that are expressed in our various traditions, understanding that a relationship of respect and support must be sustained in order to break down the walls of partition that divide Christ's church.

From this base of common beliefs we can discuss how we handle many differences. This is summarized in Article X on Board Member and Ministry Team Subscription, which states:

The members of the Board of Trustees and the Ministry Team (faculty and administrative staff) subscribe in writing to the following statements:

A. I, as far as I know my own heart, have repented from my sins against God, have received and still do rest upon Jesus Christ alone for my salvation, as He is offered to me in the gospel.

B. I also confess that by God's grace I am living in fellowship with God and that my service to the Center for Urban Theological Studies is motivated out of my desire to serve Jesus Christ in gratitude for His salvation.

C. I also confess and agree to the entirety of what is affirmed in Article VI of this Constitution and do promise always to test all I believe and practice by the rule of the Word of God. Furthermore, in areas where the teaching or practice advocated by members of the Board of Trustees or Ministry Team conflict (excluding Article VI of this Constitution), I will refrain from identifying the Center for Urban Theological Studies with that teaching or practice and I will seek with my brethren the illumination of the Spirit in the Word, working toward agreement based on the Word of God.

D. I also agree to submit to and abide by the entire Constitution, by-laws and Board policies of the Center for Urban Theological Studies.

This means that neither the faculty nor the students should leave anything they believe out of class discussion. But in those areas not covered by the CUTS doctrinal statement above, faculty members may not say that their perspective is the CUTS PERSPECTIVE, and they must agree to submit these teachings to the scrutiny of the Word of God. In other words, you are free to say, "show me from Scripture where you got that."

It also means that we agree to honor each other as Christians in the Lord who with equal integrity are seeking to work out our calling and understanding in the full light of the Word of God. Note the final statement in the "Foundations for Doing Theology-in-Ministry" above:

> We willingly submit to one another, in the Lord, always teaching, reproving, correcting and encouraging one another as we seek together to develop ways of bringing to fulfillment the whole counsel of God in our life and ministry. For this reason, we desire to establish our work with the confession of these Biblical truths that are expressed in our various traditions, understanding that a relationship of respect and support must be sustained to break down the walls of partition that divide Christ's church.

Appendix C
CUTS Statement—
Learning Together with an Open Bible

One of the unique dynamics of studying at CUTS is that you will find yourself surrounded by church leaders representing many different denominational networks and theological perspectives. You will undoubtedly find yourself hearing viewpoints and doctrines that you don't agree with. It is appropriate to ask how this should be handled. We don't want to annihilate each other through divisive debate, nor do we want to reduce what we discuss to only those things on which we agree.

CUTS itself is owned by a diverse association of churches who have united together in a common purpose which is summarized in our Constitution, Article IV:

The purpose for the Center for Urban Theological Studies is:

Section One. To serve Christ's church in Black and ethnic poor communities of the greater Philadelphia area by joining with her to refine and expand her ability for doing theology-in-ministry, through facilitating and coordinating opportunities and resources for the further training of church leaders by empowering them with knowledge, skills, and resources for effective ministry that transforms the larger urban community for Christ, and,

Section Two. In the process, to be a reconciling agent between churches in Black and ethnic poor communities and the rest of Christ's church so that the churches are enabled to share their strengths with one another and resources flow to needs.

Just what does it mean to do "theology-in-ministry"? It means that our main focus as church leaders working together at CUTS is to be on answering the challenges facing the urban church with full answers based on the Word of God. In determining to work together in "doing theology-in-ministry," a common statement of belief and commitment to labor together was summarized in our Constitution.

APPENDIX D
THE URBAN MINISTRY LEADERSHIP PROGRAM

There are two possible models for delivering the program:

First, there's the traditional model of offering courses randomly. Course instructors can't presuppose that students have had specific courses. Consequently, there is significant overlap and redundancy. It is like building a brick wall where one brick at a time is laid without giving attention to what brick you are placing. The wall looks something like this:

The "one brick at a time" learning model found in traditional programs

Second, there's a common adult learning model where, much like the layers of an onion, the courses are offered sequentially which allows the teacher to presuppose prior learning, reading, and application exercises. I like to use an onion as a model for this type of curriculum presentation.

The "onion" learning model

As in an onion, one course builds upon all the previous modules, layer after layer. Such models frequently are cohort based which means that the same group of students take all courses together in sequence. It promotes learning together in community. This model is further beneficial when there is a supervised/mentored ministry system and small group based spiritual formation system. This allows the students to progress holistically.

Over time, we designed and offered the Urban Ministry Development program which was the major offered for the last 45 credits of a 120 credit B.S. degree. These courses were:

Term I

1. Calling and Assessment
2. Dynamics of Groups at Work
3. Research Methods for Ministry
4. Cultivating a Christian World View

Term II

5. A Theology of Church in Culture
6. Urban Community Analysis
7. Doing Theology in Ministry
8. Developing a Missional Theology I

Term III

9. Developing a Missional Theology II
10. Leadership for Ministry & Mission
11. Management for Ministry & Mission
12. Project Final Presentation

This program required a final thesis in which the student identified a community need and designed a program to meet that need. Each course in this program provided a component for the final thesis.

The Ministry Project

Each one of us, created in the image of God and endowed with gifts and abilities, is responsible to sharpen our abilities and employ our talents. During this, keep in mind and heart that we serve the King of Kings, that we have nothing except what is given to us, and that God alone is worthy of all praise and honor.

As a part of the total learning experience, each student will undertake a ministry project with the approval and the supervision of the student's mentor. This project provides the vital link between the learning occurring in the classroom and the student's practice of ministry in his/her local church setting. By this means the student will bring to the classroom what he/she is experiencing in the practice of ministry at the same time that she/he is being asked to apply classroom learning into the ministry context. The best learning occurs when there is give and take in both directions.

The form of this project shall be outlined in a written contract to be signed by the student and the mentor. The project is intended to aid the student in implementing in ministry the insights gained in the program.

Rationale for the Ministry Project

The Ministry Project:

1. Is intended to be a ministry growth experience for the purpose of enabling the student to acquire ministry skills and knowledge for effective ministry.

   The ministry project is intended to provide an opportunity for the student to apply the knowledge acquired in the course work phase of the program directly to a specific area of ministry. The student will acquire skills and knowledge through experience that will both enrich him/her and benefit the ministry of which she/he is a part. Consequently, the student should identify the specific skills desired and arrange ministry experiences which will provide those skills. It is required that each student identify and find a way to work with a person already skilled in the desired area of ministry competency.

2. Is an actual operation by the student in his/her chosen area of ministry.

   An "actual operation" means that real needs of people and churches are being addressed and met by the student. The project cannot be the writing up of what you have done in the past. Nor is the project merely the writing of a report. A project is the proposing, the doing and the recording of a ministry. This means that much of the research for the project will be field research as well as surveying and collecting data on needs and previous efforts in the chosen field of ministry.

3. Focuses on a specific, unexplored or problematic area in your chosen ministry field and will contribute materially to what the church knows and is doing about the chosen field.

   The focus could be on a personal problem or behavior pattern which needs to be ministered to, a chronically perplexing issue in the church, a local congregational need, a new area of program development, the discovery of a neglected factor in the life and ministry of the church, and so on. The area of focus must be specific and narrow enough so that the student can treat it with some depth within the time limitations of the program. It must also be unexplored enough that the doing of the project will help the local ministry in which the project is conducted.

4. Is a ministry program development carried out on the foundation of, and under the constant judgment of, a significant biblical-theological base.

Actual ministry must be continuously subjected to explicit theological analysis. At the same time, during ministry the student must constantly ask whether the theological framework developed for his or her work is fully adequate (i.e., fully biblical). This means that the student should do sound and insightful exegesis and theological reflection.

5. Is a ministry program development carried out by a student fully conversant with relevant thinking, experience, and research literature in the fields of anthropology, sociology, education, theology, etc.

The student must become familiar with these areas as they relate to his/her project's area of interest. In addition, related literature and practical experience in the areas of interest must be taken into account. In order to achieve this kind of familiarity with these fields, the student must do a significant amount of reading, study and research.

6. Includes the critical evaluation of the effectiveness of the student's own ministry.

Careful goals and objectives must be formulated from the start and evaluated upon completion. It is not absolutely necessary that the program be a "success" for the project to be accepted. Insightful analysis of strengths and weaknesses of the project along with suggestions for future modifications should be included in any case.

Types of Ministry Projects

The Ministry Project will generally fall into one of the following three categories:

1. A **critical study and analysis** of a perceived problem in the community and/or church which shall include a full biblical/theological and missiological overview of the appropriate response of the church in addressing this problem.

2. A **formulation of a strategy** for solving a problem. The result will be the recommendation for the adoption of a new policy by the administration of an organization.

3. A **plan of action** to implement on his/her own initiative, at least to a great extent. This is the case where the one preparing the plan has the administrative authority to carry it out.

Questions to be asking	Chapter Topics	Content
How has God led me into this study? Why am I exploring what I am exploring?	Introduction	Life calling World view Passion for issue
What are the biblical or theological foundations for this project?	Biblical and theological rationale	Ethics Theology
How do my church and community impact this project, and how are they impacted by this project?	Context	Church profile Community profile Social relevance
What are the <u>specific</u> issues that the project will address?	Problem identification	Research
How are others approaching similar problems?	Model studies	Critical evaluation
What will I do to address the specific problem?	Ministry approach (may be more than one chapter)	Program development Analysis Methodology
What are the specifics of my plan? How will change occur?	Ministry management and mobilization	Planning Resourcing Personnel development
How did my plan work out? What were its strengths and weaknesses? What further work needs to be done?	Project evaluation	Project impacts and outcomes
How did I grow as a result of doing this project?	Personal evaluation	Personal growth assessment

The Learning Facilitator/Mentor

Each site should have a full-time person who coordinates and leads the students through all the dimensions of the program.

This includes: Introducing each unit of study or learning activity to the group and monitoring each student's progress. It also includes leading course discussion times to foster learning reflection and answering questions that come from the course units and/or reading. The facilitator also mentors the students through the spiritual formation component.

Appendix E
Krispin Report and Recommendation to the China Association of Reformed Theological Seminaries (CARTS), Fall 2017

Conferee's Expectations

1. Desire to participate in an association together to:
   a. Hold each other mutually accountable for program integrity and progress
   b. Set standards of qualifications for enrollment in all programs
   c. Share faculty and learning resources both within China and in partnership with overseas groups
   d. Have full-time CARTS staff to manage resources and program support
   e. Focus on best practices for implementation in all local programs

2. Learn how to:
   a. Set grade standards and record keeping
   b. Standardized guidelines for programs
   c. Digital library accessible to all schools
   d. Find ways to share faculty in multiple disciplines

Participant's Areas of Academic Involvement

Those attending the workshop serve in various roles in their schools:

1. New Testament – 5
2. Theology – 4
3. Administration – 3
4. Learning resources – 4

5. Counseling students – 7

6. Liaison with participating churches – 6

Age, Gender, and Degree Distribution of Enrolled Students

1. Schools with 60% women to 40% men – 3

2. Schools with a 50/50 Distribution – 3

3. Schools with majority male enrollment – 3

4. Schools with all men – 2

5. Schools with most students over 40 years of age – 2

6. Schools with most students under 40 years of age – 7

7. Majority of students are already ordained – 1

8. Schools offering both BA & Master's degree – 5

9. Schools with only a Bachelor level program – 4

10. No schools are Master's only

11. Schools with Certificate Programs – 6

Participants' Perception of Their Student Constituency

1. Most are older than 40, but age ranges from 25 to 48.

2. Come with as much as five years' preaching and teaching experience (church co-workers).

3. Desire more training both in theology and ministry.

4. Many are college graduates.

5. They plan to be pastors.

6. The training is focused on ministry in urban contexts.

7. Theologically they are orthodox.

Ten Goals for the Graduates

The students shall be:

1. Competent in hermeneutics.

2. Competent in the discipline of biblical theology.

3. Able to teach from a biblical and covenantal perspective.

4. Gospel orientated.

5. Kingdom focused in their ministry.

6. Covenant orientated in their faith.

7. Redemptive-historical in their theological perspective.

8. Spiritual in their understanding and practice of worship.

9. Able to explain and apply the "now, but not yet" understanding of the flow of redemptive history.

10. Grounded biblically and theologically for life-long learning.

Krispin's Reflections and Observations

1. All the programs are in the early stages of development. Beijing, Chengdu, and Wenzhou are the most developed.

2. Most have minimal staff and none have faculty dedicated to just teaching.

3. Currently most don't have indigenous leaders with advanced theological degrees (Th.M. and higher).

4. None of the programs have the biblical languages (Hebrew and Greek) as an integral requirement for the biblical and theological courses offered. This will limit the opportunity for doing advanced theological study in the West. Students showing promise could take the languages as an extra curriculum requirement. Wenzhou wants to incorporate the biblical languages into their program.

5. While many are preparing for pastoral ministry, there are still many who see themselves as coworkers serving in many different capacities (evangelism, Christian Education, youth and children, and counseling).

6. Almost half of the enrolled students are women whose roles in the church are still being developed even though there is a movement among many of the churches that are part of CARTS desiring to transition into male-led Presbyterian-oriented churches.

7. The staffs of the various training schools have themselves been trained in a western, academic model of theological training. This perspective hinders the group from thinking outside the box about training in the Chinese context.

8. While most of the programs see themselves as training leaders for ministry, the focus of the current training is theologically and academically focused.

9. It is likely that the training programs will grow gradually and that they won't have the capacity to have full-time faculty soon that are dedicated to teach specific courses in the program. Because the various programs don't have resident faculty, they are dependent on teachers from other places. This constrains what is offered. Consequently, courses are offered without the proper focus on a developmental concept of learning.

10. Consideration needs to be given to the development of the media packaging of learning modules where courses can be offered in a progressive prescribed ordering of courses.

11. Such an approach will require each training program to have a local learning facilitator whose responsibility it is to guide the student's learning and application into the local ministry context.

Curriculum Assumptions

1. Full-time students shall take one course each month and in the sequence listed below. This allows each course to build on the previous ones, eliminating redundancy.

2. The normal monthly cycle for full-time students shall be as follows:

    a. First week is for reading in preparation for the course.

    b. Weeks two and three classes will meet for four hours each day Monday through Friday, totaling 40 class hours.

    c. Week four is a writing week. The students shall complete all assignments.

    d. This schedule allows two full months for vacation and/or field work.

3. For part-time evening students: classes shall meet two evenings each week for 4 weeks and for 4 hours each class session. This allows for a total of 32 hours of class interaction for each course.

4. The proposed first year of study is designed to lay the groundwork of basic definitions and principles. The subsequent two years will then put flesh on those skeletal bones.

Proposed Curriculum Components

Spiritual Formation: Gospel Transformation Groups

One of the major objectives of the seminary is the growth of each seminarian into the likeness of Christ. For this purpose one day each week the morning chapel hour is to be devoted to Gospel Transformation groups of two to three students for three essential activities:

1. The reading and reflection of extensive passages of Scripture

2. Confession of sin one to another

3. Pray for each other's growth and development in the Lord

Each group will be facilitated by one of the students. What is confessed and discussed in the group is to be held in confidence by the members of the group. The following passages give the Biblical basis for this ministry of one anothering.

The Gospel Shapes and Moves Us

The gospel is the good news that Christ Jesus came into the world to save sinners. The gospel says that we are so sinful, lost, and helpless that only the life and death of the Son of God can save us. But the gospel is not just the way to enter the kingdom—it is the new way to do everything and to grow every step. *The gospel tells us that we are more sinful than we ever knew, but more loved and accepted in Christ than we ever dared to hope.* Therefore the gospel gives us enormous power to admit our flaws and sins. It gives us an entirely new self-image that is not based in our performance or comparison with others. Therefore we seek to continually preach the gospel to ourselves, then to the church and the world.

When the gospel is at work in us, it gives us new freedom, new power, and new relationships. It creates a gospel-shaped community in our midst. Through lives of daily repentance, we will be delivered from self-righteousness, pride, competitiveness, and party spirit. The fruits of repentance will be seen in personal change, biblical conflict resolution, sacrificial love, compassion, intimacy, and honesty.

> For the grace of God that brings salvation has appeared to all men. It teaches us to say "No" to ungodliness and worldly passions, and to live self-controlled, upright and godly lives in this present age, while we wait for the blessed hope—the glorious appearing of our great God and Savior,

Jesus Christ, who gave himself for us to redeem us from all wickedness and to purify for himself a people that are his very own, eager to do what is good. These, then, are the things you should teach. Encourage and rebuke with all authority. Do not let anyone despise you. (Titus 2:11–14)

Christ came not only to pay the penalty for our sins, he came also to transform us through cleansing into Christlikeness. See also Ephesians 2:8–10:

> For it is by grace you have been saved, through faith—and this not from yourselves, it is the gift of God—not by works, so that no one can boast. For we are God's workmanship, created in Christ Jesus to do good works, which God prepared in advance for us to do.

We see this also clearly in Romans 6:1–14:

> What shall we say, then? Shall we go on sinning so that grace may increase? By no means! We died to sin; how can we live in it any longer? Or don't you know that all of us who were baptized into Christ Jesus were baptized into his death? We were therefore buried with him through baptism into death in order that, just as Christ was raised from the dead through the glory of the Father, we too may live a new life. If we have been united with him like this in his death, we will certainly also be united with him in his resurrection. For we know that our old self was crucified with him so that the body of sin might be done away with, that we should no longer be slaves to sin—because anyone who has died has been freed from sin. Now if we died with Christ, we believe that we will also live with him. For we know that since Christ was raised from the dead, he cannot die again; death no longer has mastery over him. The death he died, he died to sin once for all; but the life he lives, he lives to God. In the same way, count yourselves dead to sin but alive to God in Christ Jesus. Therefore do not let sin reign in your mortal body so that you obey its evil desires. Do not offer the parts of your body to sin, as instruments of wickedness, but rather offer yourselves to God, as those who have been brought from death to life; and offer the parts of your body to him as instruments of righteousness. For sin shall not be your master, because you are no under law, but under grace.

This great truth is further explained in Colossians 3:1–17:

> Since, then, you have been raised with Christ, set your hearts on things above, where Christ is seated at the right hand of God. Set your minds on things above, not on earthly things. For you died, and your life is now hidden with Christ in God. When Christ, who is your life, appears, then you also will appear with him in glory. Put to death, therefore, whatever

belongs to your earthly nature: sexual immorality, impurity, lust, evil desires and greed, which is idolatry. Because of these, the wrath of God is coming. You used to walk in these ways, in the life you once lived. But now you must rid yourselves of all such things as these: anger, rage, malice, slander, and filthy language from your lips. Do not lie to each other, since you have taken off your old self with its practices and have put on the new self, which is being renewed in knowledge in the image of its Creator. Here there is no Greek or Jew, circumcised or uncircumcised, barbarian, Scythian, slave or free, but Christ is all, and is in all. Therefore, as God's chosen people, holy and dearly loved, clothe yourselves with compassion, kindness, humility, gentleness and patience. Bear with each other and forgive whatever grievances you may have against one another. Forgive as the Lord forgave you. And over all these virtues put on love, which binds them all together in perfect unity. Let the peace of Christ rule in your hearts, since as members of one body you were called to peace. And be thankful. Let the word of Christ dwell in you richly as you teach and admonish one another with all wisdom, and as you sing psalms, hymns and spiritual songs with gratitude in your hearts to God. And whatever you do, whether in word or deed, do it all in the name of the Lord Jesus, giving thanks to God the Father through him.

Note the language Paul uses here:

1. Because of Christ's work in us we are to "put to death . . . whatever belongs to your earthly nature" (3:5), and,

2. We are to clothe ourselves with "compassion, kindness, humility, gentleness and patience. Bear with each other and forgive whatever grievances you may have against one another. Forgive as the Lord forgave you" (3:12–13).

In other words, we are called to actively engage in this change to our sinful lives. The path to this is found in verse 16 through three means:

1. Let the word of Christ dwell in you richly (the study and meditation upon God's Word),

2. as you teach and admonish one another with all wisdom (shepherding care within the body of Christ), and

3. as you sing psalms, hymns and spiritual songs with gratitude in your hearts to God (worship).

This dynamic is what we call "fellowship"—the building up of one another in Christ.

What Is Fellowship?

Fellowship, at its core meaning, is the pure communion between the persons of the Godhead; Father, Son, and Holy Spirit, revealed fully in the person and work of Christ. We see this in First John 1:1–4 and 5–10.

> That which was from the beginning, which we have heard, which we have seen with our eyes, which we have looked at and our hands have touched—this we proclaim concerning the Word of life. The life appeared; we have seen it and testify to it, and we proclaim to you the eternal life, which was with the Father and has appeared to us. We proclaim to you what we have seen and heard, so that you also may have fellowship with us. And our fellowship is with the Father and with his Son, Jesus Christ. We write this to make our joy complete.

Note:

1. What Christ reveals is his life with the Father before he became a man (1:1).

2. This life is revealed so that we too can be a part of this fellowship.

3. This fellowship is not just for the here and now, but it is eternal.

But what does this fellowship look like for us? Look now at verses 5–10:

> This is the message we have heard from him and declare to you: God is light; in him there is no darkness at all. If we claim to have fellowship with him yet walk in the darkness, we lie and do not live by the truth. But if we walk in the light, as he is in the light, we have fellowship with one another, and the blood of Jesus, his Son, purifies us from all sin. If we claim to be without sin, we deceive ourselves and the truth is not in us. If we confess our sins, he is faithful and just and will forgive us our sins and purify us from all unrighteousness. If we claim we have not sinned, we make him out to be a liar and his word has no place in our lives.

Note:

1. God is light and in him is no darkness at all (1:5). In other words, God is holy and there is no sin in him and in his fellowship.

2. John says this truth has three profound implications:

   a. First, if we claim we are a part of this fellowship and yet we walk in sin, we are liars and we do not live in this truth (1:6).

   b. But also, if we claim to be without sin, we deceive ourselves and the truth is not in us (1:8).

   c. Finally, if we claim that we have not sinned, we make God out to be a liar and his word has no place in our lives (1:10).

3. This chain of thinking would create an impossible dilemma for us if this is the end of the story. After all, we are sinners and are therefore unworthy to have fellowship with the triune God.

4. But the story is not complete without verses 7 and 9.

   a. If we walk in the light as Christ is in the light we have fellowship one with another and the Blood of Christ cleanses us from all sin.

   b. See John 3:19–21:

> This is the verdict: Light has come into the world, but men loved darkness instead of light because their deeds were evil. Everyone who does evil hates the light, and will not come into the light for fear that his deeds will be exposed. But whoever lives by the truth comes into the light, so that it may be seen plainly that what he has done has been done through God.

      i. Sinners can't stand the light and therefore hide from the light.

      ii. But believers love the light because it exposes their sin and it allows God to do his great work of cleansing them from all their sin.

      iii. This work can only be done by God Himself.

   c. But how does this cleansing work occur in the life of the believer? Verse 9 makes it clear: "If we confess our sins, he is faithful and just and will forgive us our sins and purify us from all unrighteousness."

      i. Confession of sin leads to God's forgiveness, but also,

      ii. It leads to cleansing from our sin. This is what was referred to above in Romans 6 and Colossians 3.

Supervised Ministry Experience—The Spiral of Ministry Development

Pastoral Leadership

———

Small group or ministry team leadership

———

Preaching and teaching

———

Evangelism and discipleship

———

New believers witnessing in their friendship and family webs of relationship

———

Serving in specific ministries of helps

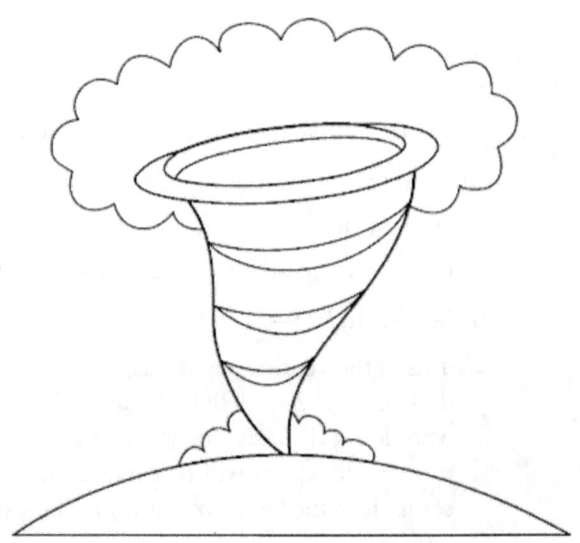

The Being-Knowing-Doing paradigm

1. The faithfulness/fruitfulness principle
   a. Implications of this for training and the ordination process?
      i. The church needs to define an ordination process
         1) A new understanding of age requirement
         2) Training relevant to process
         3) Stages of the process
            a) Under care
            b) Supervised ministry development
            c) Licensed to preach within the presbytery/district
            d) Internship
            e) Ordination when there is a specific call to office/ministry
      ii. Assessment should be in all three areas
      iii. Ministry evaluations from ministers and practitioners
         1) Interviews of the same and by peers and friends on character
         2) Evaluations of internships
         3) Examinations in biblical and theological areas

Appendix F
A Curriculum Proposal to CARTS (2021)

Three-year M.Div. Curriculum Proposal

1. **<u>Practical Theology (31 hours)</u>**

   A. Objectives:

   1) The student shall demonstrate a clear understanding of the transforming gospel of Christ both for ministry and life.

   2) The student shall be able to articulate his/her calling to ministry.

   3) The student shall develop a plan for growing into Christlikeness for a lifetime (being, knowing, and doing).

   4) The student shall be able to articulate the mission of Christ's church for today and to lead in engaging this ministry.

   5) The student shall have involvement in and ability to engage in the discipleship of those not yet followers of Christ and those both in spiritual infancy and seasoned maturity.

   6) The student shall have an understanding of the ministry that he/she is preparing for and have a plan for developing it.

   B. Courses:

   1) Calling and Assessment

   2) Spiritual Formation—The Gospel Shapes and Moves Us

   3) The Mission and Ministry of the Church

   4) Evangelism and Discipleship

   5) Pastoral Care and Biblical Counseling

   or

   Sermon Preparation

6) Worship (1 hour)

7) Ministry Specializations (5 courses in each area)

    a) Pastoral Ministry

    b) Church Planting

    c) Youth and College Ministry

    d) Educational Ministry in the Church

    e) Biblical Counseling

Preaching a sermon or developing a teaching lesson/series are good ways to ascertain knowledge in biblical and theological areas and to demonstrate gifts for ministry. Generally, these are just as effective in determining competency as are papers.

2. **<u>Biblical Studies (30 hours)</u>**

    A. Objectives:

      1) Program focuses on the disciplines of hermeneutics, exegetical theology, and biblical theology.

      2) The student shall to be able to exegete specific scripture passages and to apply them into life and ministry.

      3) The student shall be able to understand a passage's place in redemptive history and to explain/teach/apply the passages to the people of God.

      4) The student shall be able to articulate/teach/preach from a covenantal and kingdom perspective.

      5) The student shall nderstand and articulate our place today in the redemptive-historical plan of God.

    B. Courses:

    1) Introduction to Biblical Theology

    2) Hermeneutics

    3) OT History and Theology I: Pentateuch

    4) OT History and Theology II: The Period of the Judges and Kings

    5) OT History and Theology III: The Prophets and Intertestamental Period

   6) NT History and Theology I: The Life and Ministry of Christ

   7) NT History and Theology II: The Acts of the Apostles and Epistles

   8) Eschatology and Spiritual Warfare

   9) Capstone Courses:

      a) Preaching and Biblical Theology

      b) Studies in Biblical Theology

3. <u>Systematic and Historical Theology (33 hours)</u>

A. Objectives:

   1) The student shall be able to teach/preach the full teaching of Scripture and to apply it to all areas of life.

   2) The student shall be able to exegete one's own culture and community and to articulate God's calling to serve in that context.

   3) The student shall be able to explain and engage the various world and life perspectives in the surrounding cultures.

   4) The student shall be able to articulate/evaluate/engage the various positions held by believers and unbelievers down through the centuries.

   5) The student shall be able to identify and engage the various ethical challenges in the surrounding culture.

B. Courses:

   1) Introduction to Theology: The Doctrine of the Word/Revelation

   2) Systematic Theology I: The Doctrine of God and Man

   3) Systematic Theology II: The Doctrine of Salvation

   4) Systematic Theology III: The Doctrine of the Holy Spirit

   5) Church History I: The History of Christianity in the West

   6) Church History II: The History of Christianity in China

   7) Introduction to Apologetics

   8) Developing a Christian Worldview

   9) The Church in a Changing Culture: Understanding and Engaging Our World of Change

10) Engaging Chinese Culture and Religions

11) Making Ethical Decisions

Total hours: 94

Note: Only the Wenzhou seminary offers Greek and Hebrew. Students desiring to study abroad for an advanced degree will likely need to gain Greek and Hebrew competency through other means—online courses or tutorial.

THREE-YEAR CURRICULUM PLAN

<u>Year One</u>

1. Calling and Assessment for Ministry
2. Spiritual Formation: The Gospel Shapes and Moves Us
3. The Mission and Ministry of the Church
4. Introduction to Theology: The Doctrine of the Word/Revelation
5. Introduction to Biblical Theology
6. Hermeneutics
7. Introduction to Apologetics
8. Developing A Christian Worldview
9. Old Testament History and Theology I
10. Old Testament History and Theology II

Total hours: 30

<u>Year Two</u>

1. Church History I: The History of Christianity in the West
2. Evangelism and Discipleship
3. Pastoral Care and Biblical Theology
4. The Church in a Changing Culture: Understanding and Engaging Our World of Change
5. Engaging Chinese Culture and Religions
6. New Testament History and Theology I

   7. New Testament History and Theology II

   8. Systematic Theology I: The Doctrine of God and Man

   9. Systematic Theology II: The Doctrine of Salvation

  10. Church History in the Western World II

Total hours: 30

Year Three

1. Systematic Theology III: The Doctrine of the Holy Spirit

2. Church History II: The History of Christianity in China

3. Capstone: Studies in Biblical Theology

4. Eschatology and Spiritual Warfare

5. Capstone: Preaching and Biblical Theology

6. Worship (1 hour)

7. Making Ethical Decisions

8. Ministry Specialization Courses—preparing for future ministry in: Pastoral Ministry, Church Planting, Youth and College Ministry, Educational Ministry in the Church, or Biblical Counseling (5 courses)

Total hours: 34

Total overall program credits: 94

Year Four

The optional fourth year can be used to give the student additional experience in ministry through a mentored internship in a local church setting under an experienced pastor.

Learning facilitators

There are three essential threads of ministry and theological training:

1. Gospel transformation of personal character through spiritual transformation (Being).

2. Ministry skill development (Doing). Serving in congregational or campus ministry through progression through the various stages of ministry skill development outlined in the spiral of ministry development.

3. Course learning (Knowing). This is the easiest one of the three to deliver. The other two are more challenging, requiring more direct student interaction with a peer learning group, a mentor and a ministry supervisor.

General program assumptions:

1. Effective learning involves developing critical thinking skills whereby the student examines one's own beliefs and practices by testing them in the light of Scripture.

2. It also involves knowing and analyzing other positions. It is not enough to know what you believe but it is essential to know how and why you believe this and also learning from critical critiques by others holding other position. To study only what you already believe is indoctrination but it is not critical thinking.

3. We listen and learn best when we are challenged with new and/or different thinking and beliefs. This forces us to reflect more critically on our own beliefs.

4. Learning in a cohort with other learners enlarges the student-teacher dimension in that everyone is both a learner and a teacher. This requires building trust and respect relationships. Thus, good learning is always collaborative and dialogical.

5. In a formal learning context such learning requires a learning facilitator who has himself/herself has been through the training process. This person guides the students through their studies.

6. The facilitator must be willing to lead by submitting his/her own beliefs, values, and practices for scrutiny by others involved in the cohort.

7. Theological education requires a critical consciousness of one's own beliefs and practices in ministry.

8. Ministry training requires developing and sharpening one's own ministry skills with an eye on sharpening one's sense of calling and placement from God.

9. At the beginning of each year the facilitator shall conduct a workshop where each student shall write a learning contract for the year in all three curriculum components (Being-Doing-Knowing) to identify specific areas of growth in life, ministry and thought. This contract shall be the basis for the evaluation of a student's progress

throughout the year. The student, facilitator and ministry supervisor shall all review and sign the contract.

10. In cohort learning we want to see the student grow from being dependent on others for growth, to independence in managing one's own progress to the final point of mutual interdependence where strengths are shared, character is transformed, weaknesses are addressed.

11. This program involves learning through individual study and reflection, in mentorship under a learning facilitator, through involvement in study groups with other students, and through ministry projects both individually and in groups.

Paulo Freire was a Brazilian educator who developed an adult reading literacy training. His key learning resources are:

The Pedagogy of the Oppressed

1. Education for a critical consciousness

2. Pedagogy in Process (Letters to the Education Minister in Guinea Bissau in West Africa on adult literacy training)

Key concepts from Freire:

1. A key concept in his method is "conscientization"—the raising of one's critical consciousness as to who he/she is and for what purpose he/she is here for.

2. Freire was a Roman Catholic who based his literacy training concept on his understanding on "naming" as it's found in Genesis 2:18–20. This passage tells the account of the assignment that God gave Adam in the Garden to name the animals and all things in the garden as created by God.

   a. While Genesis doesn't tell us the name Adam gave we can be sure he named them in reference to God the Creator and Lord over all. We get insight into naming in Job 38–39 where animals are described in terms of their physical characteristics and usefulness.

   b. Freire understood that everything changed when mankind fell into sin. Sin renames everything now in terms of humans owning and lording over all.

   c. In redemption we must question the names given in human's fallen condition and rename them back to God as Creator-Lord over all.

d. In literacy training Freire began by having the students name their world where they lived, worked, played, etc. He used slides to do this. He would ask the students to tell him what they saw in the pictures. He would then probe their definitions and description of what they said. He would get them to question the names by which they labeled things. He would then push them to rename them in terms of a higher purpose of justice. He would use the stories they told, using their labels and definitions to teach them to read. This method proved to be highly effective in teaching adults to read.

e. But Freire's understanding of sin is also informative. He alleged that sin isn't just selfishness, self-centeredness whereby we want to do our own thing. It lead him to believe that humans wanted also to be everyone else's Lord. Hence, in his basic understanding, sin is oppression. This sin is what leads to strife and alienation in the world.

f. Because of the radical nature of his thought Freire was forced to live in exile for the latter part of his life. But this only meant that his influence only grew throughout the world.

g. He also made a major contribution in his definition of the "banking concept of education." Basically stated: in the traditional lecture-oriented classroom, knowledge goes from the instructor's notes to the student's notes without going through either of their minds. Studies have shown that students don't remember 75% of what was said in a lecture one day later if listening was the only means of learning. Retention goes up greatly when the students use the knowledge immediately either through dialogue in a learning group or by an application activity. The models in this proposal seeks to provide that variety of learning activities. It should also be noted that students will learn more from reading and reflection than they would in only listening to a lecture.

These thoughts serve as a backdrop for this proposal.

The Learning Facilitator

It is noted elsewhere that one of the challenges facing the CARTS schools is the lack of resident faculty in the various training areas. Most staff at the schools are serving in some administrative function also lack advanced degrees in theology or in ministry. Given the need for program resources it is likely that this will continue for 10–20 years if not longer. With that in mind this proposal proposes a shared model where **CARTS will for the foreseeable future will be one school with multiple locations.**

Two Models of delivering the program:

1. **The traditional model** of offering courses randomly. Course instructors can't presuppose that students have had specific courses. Consequently, there is significant overlap or redundancy. It is like building a brick wall where one brick at a time is laid without giving attention to what brick you are placing. The wall looks something like this:

The "one brick at a time" learning model found in traditional programs

2. **A common adult learning model** where much like the layers of an onion the courses are offered sequentially which allows the teacher to presuppose prior learning, reading, and application exercises.

The "onion" learning model

Such models frequently are cohort based which means that the same group of students take all courses together in sequence. This model is further benefited when there is a supervised/mentored ministry system and small group based spiritual formation system. This allows the students to progress holistically.

Role of the facilitator:

1. Each site should have a full-time person who coordinates and leads the students through all the dimensions of the program. This includes:

a. Introducing each unit of study or learning activity to the group.

b. Monitoring each student's progress.

c. Leading course discussion times to foster learning reflection

d. Answering questions that come from the course units and/or reading.

e. Mentoring students through the spiritual formation component

f. Working with site ministry supervision for the student's as they serve in various capacities in local ministry settings.

g. Coordinating the student program evaluation process.

h. This team shall plan and conduct an annual training week for the training and networking of the Learning facilitators.

2. Other administrative personnel needed (can be part time at each site or full time serving the network as a whole. This includes but is not restricted to:

a. A registrar to record grads and monitor progress toward completion of all program requirements.

b. A Dean of Program Components. This person serves the various sites with program evaluation and staff training. This person should report to the CARTS board.

c. A Curriculum Team Leader who shall keep the curriculum course development moving forward in a timely way. The curriculum team itself should be made up of five to seven people working at writing the program and course units. Team members shall come from these areas:

    i.   Theology

    ii.   Biblical-Theological

    iii.   Practical Ministry

    iv.   Learning media resources

    v.   Learning facilitators for each site

    vi.   Spiritual formation

    vii. Ministry skill development

    viii.A financial and fund-raising person. This project will need significant financial and personnel resources. One seminary with multiple locations could pool financial resources to ensure that resources are provided where and when needed. This project will likely need to find significant financial sources of funding. These should come first from the churches of the various church networks participating in the project, but also from outside resources that may be identified and cultivated. Such sources should include The China Partnership of the USA PCA, City to City of Redeemer Church in NYC, and Third Millenium Ministries out of Orlando, Florida.

(SAMPLE COURSE DESCRIPTIONS)

The following are taken from the catalog of Westminster Seminary; some have been edited to fit the preceding curriculum proposal. Others came from The Leadership and Ministry Preparation program (LAMP) of CityNet Ministries in Philadelphia.

APOLOGETICS

Apologetics is a theological discipline that seeks to defend and commend the Christian faith. The apologetic tradition of Westminster attempts to apply Reformed theology to the challenges that confront Christianity and the church. Apologetics is an indispensable preparation for gospel ministry and for evangelism. To that end, the Apologetics curriculum enables students:

- To understand biblical religion as a world-and-life view, rather than a set of isolated truths

- To develop arguments which address the deepest levels of various worldviews

- To articulate biblical principles for the defense and commendation of the gospel of Jesus Christ in evangelism

- To understand the patterns and cultural trends of our times

- To develop answers to some of the most frequent challenges raised against Christian faith

- To know something of the history of thought, Western and non-Western

- To be familiar with some of the most significant apologists throughout history

- To articulate the relationship between faith and reason

Introduction to Apologetics

Purpose: To introduce students to Christian apologetics

- To learn the art of Christian persuasion.

- To learn how to lift up Christ and give reasons for the hope that we have (1 Peter 3:15)

- To develop tools in order to understand the surrounding culture.

Topics covered include the biblical basis for apologetics, developing a world and life view, the issue of meaning, covenantal, engaging contemporary culture, and highlights in the history of apologetics.

We will give special attention to the problem of meaning, the problem of evil, world religions (including Islam), science and faith, reason and revelation, and aesthetics.

Old Testament

Nothing is more foundational to Christian ministry than a full-orbed knowledge and embrace of the gospel. The Old Testament department is committed to teaching the first thirty-nine books of the Bible, with all the aspects entailed, as the anticipation of the glorious climactic fulfillment of redemption in Jesus Christ.

To this end, the Old Testament curriculum enables students:

- To acquire a reading knowledge of biblical Hebrew

- To acquire a knowledge of the content of the Old Testament

- To grapple with the challenges of biblical interpretation

- To evaluate the ways in which the Old Testament has been interpreted in the past

- To perceive the unity of the Old and New Testaments and the hermeneutical significance of their unity

- To understand and value the historical context in which God gave his redemptive revelation, how it began in the Old Testament period and then culminated in the glorious and extraordinary climax to that history in Christ and his work in Christ as interpreted in the New Testament

- To identify the major biblical-theological themes of the Old Testament and to recognize their importance for understanding the gospel

- To develop skill in understanding and applying each of the books of the Old Testament

- To learn to communicate the gospel through the Old Testament

- To be encouraged to embrace the gospel in continuing and vital ways through the glory of God's self-disclosure and to fear the Lord and love him with the whole heart.

OT 131 Biblical Theology I

Purpose: To show how responsible interpretation and application of any biblical text does not begin with the question "How do I apply this passage to my life?" but with "How does this passage connect to the great narrative of redemption which climaxes in the gospel, the story of Christ, and his people?"

Topics covered include the nature of the Bible and its coherence; continuities and discontinuities in various major themes, such as the kingdom of God, definitions of the people of God, the Spirit and the New Covenant; the centrality of the gospel in application.

Old Testament History and Theology I
Purpose:

- To provide an introduction to the theology of the Pentateuch

- To engage in the exegesis of selected passages from the Pentateuch with particular attention to their relationship to ancient Near Eastern literature, the theology of the Pentateuch as a whole, and to the history of redemption as it reaches its climax in the gospel Topics covered include the narrative structure of the Bible, the Pentateuch and the history of redemption, Genesis 1–3 as an entry point to biblical theology, and the book of Exodus.

Old Testament History and Theology II
Purpose:

- To explore the relationship among literature, history, and theology in the books of Deuteronomy through Ezra/Nehemiah

- To provide a knowledge of the content of this section of canon

- To give a biblical-theological framework for applying these books in life and ministry.

In addition to laying out the theology and content of each of these books, we will cover such topics as the relationship of Deuteronomy to the other books. Additional topics covered include OT historiography; OT theology; the relationship between revelation, history, and theology; and covenant.

Old Testament History and Theology III
Purpose:

- To explore the relationship among literature, history, and theology in the books of Job, Psalms and the Prophets

- To provide a knowledge of the content of this section of canon

- To give a biblical-theological framework for applying these books in life and ministry.

In addition to laying out the theology and content of each of these books, we will cover such topics as the relationship of Deuteronomy to these books. Additional topics covered include OT historiography; OT theology; the relationship between revelation, history, and theology; and covenant, and the coming of the Messiah.

NEW TESTAMENT

The New Testament is the account of the presence of the kingdom of heaven, and centers in the person of Jesus Christ. This is the cornerstone for all Christian ministries. The New Testament department is committed to teaching the New Testament as the full revelation of the covenant of God's grace in Jesus Christ.

To this end, the New Testament curriculum enables students:

- To acquire a reading knowledge of New Testament Greek

- To understand and value the historical context in which God accomplished his work in Christ, and through which he gave us the New Testament

- To perceive the unity of the Old and New Testaments and the hermeneutical significance thereof

- To grapple with the challenges of biblical interpretation

- To recognize major biblical-theological themes of the New Testament and their importance for understanding the biblical message

- To evaluate the ways in which the New Testament has been interpreted in the past

- To develop skill in understanding and applying each of the books of the New Testament

Biblical Hermeneutics

Old and New Testaments Purpose: To grow in skill in understanding, interpreting, and applying the Bible.

Topics covered include prolegomena to biblical interpretation, principles and practice of biblical interpretation, and the question of hermeneutics in the historical-critical tradition.

New Testament Biblical Theology I & II

Purpose: To show how responsible interpretation and application of any biblical text does not begin with the question "How do I apply this passage to my life?" but with "How does this passage connect to the great narrative of redemption which climaxes in the gospel, the story of Christ, and his people?"

Topics covered include the nature of the Bible and its coherence; continuities and discontinuities in various major themes, such as the kingdom of God, definitions of the people of God, the Spirit and the New Covenant; the centrality of the gospel in application first in the Gospels, then in Acts and the Epistles.

The Gospel Moves and Shapes Us: The gospel is the good news that Christ Jesus came into the world to save sinners. The gospel says that we are so sinful, lost, and helpless that only the life, death and resurrection of the Son of God can save us. But the gospel is not just the way to enter the kingdom—it is the new way to do everything and to grow every step. ***The gospel tells us that we are more sinful than we ever knew, but more loved and accepted in Christ than we ever dared to hope.*** Therefore the gospel gives us enormous power to admit our flaws and sins. It gives us an entirely new self-image that is not based in our performance or comparison with others. Therefore we seek to continually preach the gospel to ourselves, then to the church and the world. When the gospel is at work in us, it gives us new freedom, new power, and new relationships. It creates a gospel-shaped community in our midst. Through lives of daily repentance we will be delivered from self-righteousness, pride, competitiveness, and party spirit. The fruits of repentance will be seen in personal change, biblical conflict resolution, sacrificial love, compassion, intimacy and honesty.

Making Disciples (Units: 3)

Course Description:

Jesus commanded his disciples to "make disciples of the nations." Disciples making disciples involved two basic phases: bringing people to a place that they were ready to confess Christ and be baptized, and teaching them to walk in obedience to the teaching of Jesus. Both phases are the church's work of discipleship.

This course will seek to understand the church's calling to make disciples in this more biblical way. We will learn to think of evangelism through our church communities in a way that leads naturally into the discipleship of the new believer and ongoing discipleship of all believers.

Course Objectives:

Upon successfully completing this course, students should be able to:

1. Articulate the approach to evangelism and discipleship taught in the Great Commission.

2. Demonstrate the ability to be a spiritual midwife and to help others discern their spiritual journeys through the preparation and presentation of case studies.

3. Explain how the Gospel is the fundamental biblical resource for the entire process of making disciples.

4. Learn how to participate in and lead a Gospel Transformation Group for discipling others in the Gospel walk.

5. Grow in your ability to interpret and apply Scripture to your life.

Calling and Assessment

Course Description:

This course provides an in-depth study of the CALL to the gospel ministry. It will examine the biblical, theological, historical and contemporary basis of calling as well as its practical application in the life and ministry of today's present and emerging "Servant-Leaders." This course is designed to enhance leadership competence, confidence and clarity in discerning the call and development to pastoral ministry, holistic ministry and Christian service at large. Emphasis is on awareness of a personal Calling to the Pastoral Ministry, Holistic Gospel Ministry and Life-Long Learning and Development.

Student Learning Outcomes:

Upon completion of this course, students should be able to:

1. Clearly discern and define his/her specific ministry gifts and personal calling to the pastoral or gospel ministry.

2. Envision and articulate a strategy and plan for lifelong development and learning for effective ministry.

3. Communicate an in-depth understanding and appreciation of the diversity of Holistic Gospel Ministry and the need for practical application.

MANAGEMENT FOR MISSION AND MINISTRY

Course Description:

In this course you will be introduced to the process of strategic planning and ministry development. After introducing the planning process we will explore the five major ministry areas in the church: 1. Evangelism, 2. Discipleship or Christian Education, 3. Fellowship, 4. Worship, and service (The Ministry of mercy and justice). While we are doing this you be engaged in small groups of four to five students to identify, analyze, and plan a strategy for developing a ministry within the local church or network. You will operate as the leaders of the network who oversee the work of the entire church. Finally, in class, each group will present their plan along with a full biblical rationale using powerpoint. Each student must present a portion of the report.

Because of the significant reading requirement for the course each team will begin with each team member reading one of the required books and writing a summary of the learning for ministry that they gleaned from their reading. This summary will be given to the other members of the group and it will be discussed within the group. This learning will serve as the foundation for the project.

Course Objectives:

1. To understand the mission and ministry of the church

2. To learn the strategic planning process through a simulation exercise.

3. To explore the parameters and focus of each of the five strategic areas of church ministry.

4. To understand the internal and external dynamics impacting and influencing ministry change and development.

5. To understand and develop strategies for addressing problems and barriers.

6. To understand how to evaluate progress and make adjustments in your plan.

7. To understand the role of the leader within the church and to develop a plan for how you will function as a leader in the unfolding of your project.

8. To practice team ministry

9. To development plan for a church ministry

10. To articulate a theological foundation for the ministry.

Reading groups: The class is to be organized into groups of five students. Each student will read *one* of the five required books and give a full report on the book to the other students in the reading group. Using this means all five members of the group will benefit from the reading of the five books. These five will become the ministry planning group later in the course to plan and present a ministry development project. The five areas of ministry represented in this reading are: Evangelism, Discipleship, Christian Education, Fellowship, and Worship.

Group projects: Organize class into groups of four, and if necessary, three or five. Each group will choose a ministry for which they will develop a strategic ministry plan to develop or implement. It must be within one of five areas of ministry outlined above. (Students might want to group by the ministries that they are involved in: Sunday school; high school/middle school youth; young adults, including college; Preaching/worship; etc.)

The plan should generally follow the outline presented in class for Strategic Planning. The focus could be centered on improving the existing ministry, better involving a team approach, or the planning and/or implementation of a new ministry.

Each group will have 20 minutes to make their presentation and they must use powerpoint media for this purpose. Each team member must present.

Only Luke is with me. Get Mark and bring him with you, because he is helpful to me in my ministry. I sent Tychicus to Ephesus. When you come, bring the cloak that I left with Carpus at Troas, and my scrolls, especially the parchments. (2 Tim. 4:11–13)

Appendix G
How Ministry has Changed in my 57 Years of Service in Philadelphia

1. Shifting Demographics

    a. Population explosion

        i. World population growth

Time of Christ:	250,000,000
1776	1 Billion
World War I	2 Billion
World War II	3 Billion
1964	4 Billion
1985	5 Billion
1995	6 Billion
2008	6,785,728,850
2025	8,674,927,348 (projected)
2035	10,023,000,000 (projected)

       ii. Urbanization of the world—percentage living in cities

1800	3%
1900	14%
1950	33%
1980	40%
2000	Approaching 50%
2025	60%

Note 1: Urbanization % of USA population has reached 79%, 19th in the world.

Note 2: China today has 49 cities of more than one million in population; India, 43 cities.

   iii. USA population by decade

1940	132,164,569
1950	151,325,798 (+14.5%)
1960	178,554,966 (+8.5%)
1970	203,302,031 (+13.4%)
1980	226,545,805 (+11.4%)
1990	248,709,873 (+9.8%)
2000	281,421,906 (+13.2%)
2008	303,000,000
2050	Over 450,000,000 (projected)

   iv. Philadelphia population

	METRO AREA	**CITY**
1930	3.3 million	1.95 million
1940	3.4 million	1.93 million
1950	3.9 million	2.07 million
1960	4.6 million	2.0 million
1970	5.1 million	1.95 million
1980	5.02 million	1.68 million
1990	5.2 million	1.57 million
2000	5.4 million	1.448 million

b. Racial/ethnic diversification—By 2050 Caucasians will be only 47% of the population; Latinos (29%), African Americans (13%), and Asians (9%). 27% of the population will be foreign born, up from the current level of 11%.

c. The American love affair with the automobile:

   i. From 1997 to 2007 the number of cars in the Pennsylvania side of the Philadelphia Metro area increased by 500,000.

   ii. Philadelphia doesn't have the necessary road system to sustain this type of growth in automobiles.

   iii. The need for a region wide light rail system utilizing the many abandoned train beds distributed throughout the region.

d. The internet and the work from home movement—living in a virtual world.

e. The paradigm of how suburbs are created has shifted dramatically since 1950.

f. Urbanization of the suburbs—the 20-minute commute rule; the emergence of the Edge City; what you'll see in the next 20–30 years; what are the limits of sprawl?

g. And suburbanization of the city

h. The city continues to give its people to the inner suburbs; the inner suburbs give its people to the outer suburbs.

i. Beginning in the mid-1990s, we began to see a movement of suburbanites returning to live in the city—the Center City condo phenomenon, students and first career people, and the influx of immigrant populations coming to the city.

j. The myth of "best locations" for new churches—plant on the frontiers of the new housing suburban developments.

k. Rather, plant in the places of greatest change, which most frequently are found in the city.

l. The disappearance of the intergenerational church and the disconnect of the new emerging generation.

m. With the rapid tides of change in urban and metropolitan areas, the life cycle of churches is shrinking. We are now in the era of one-generation churches.

n. It's crucial that church planters develop a theology of place—Jim Boice: "This People, This Time, This Place."

o. Dwight Smith: Providing every man, woman, and child with repeated opportunities to hear, see, and respond to the gospel of Jesus Christ.

p. The decline of the neighborhood/community-based church to the regional, mega, seeker church phenomenon.

q. Given the neighborhood and township configuration of the Philadelphia Metro area, we need to return to smaller, community-rooted churches to bring incarnational ministry close at hand to people who are increasingly unlikely to enter the doors of the church.

r. Watch for the emergence of the house church for reaching people on the fringe and the disenfranchised.

s. With this trend will come growth in the number of bi-vocational pastors.

t. Changing paradigms of funding church plants—the high-cost model needs to change.

2. **"The church is always just one generation from extinction" (Eddie Gibbs).** That's why it's crucial that we have an intentional strategy for reaching and mobilizing the emerging generation (18–34-year-olds).

   a. 28% of Philadelphia's population are between the ages of 18 and 34.

   b. There are over 300,000 residents of the Philadelphia region attending college.

   c. Yet, Philly has a very low rate of retention of its college grads. This has to do with the availability of viable jobs in their field.

   d. For most churches this generation is absent today.

   e. Yet 95% of church attenders came to faith in Christ before the age of 30.

   f. There are several problems that need to be explored and understood:

      i. For the first time, this generation is living in affinity neighborhoods other than near campuses.

      ii. The mile radius around City Hall has 50% emerging population living there.

      iii. "Friends" are clustering as never before.

      iv. Marriage is being delayed and even ignored.

      v. The "normal" family is now not married.

      vi. Outreach by this generation to this generation still goes on, but if it follows preceding generations, it will be limited to a season.

      vii. We have done poorly in continuing evangelism after we "settled down."

      viii. Most Christians turn inward.

   g. The church has failed miserably in incorporating college grads into the life and ministry of the church.

   h. Churches are too often closed shops for leadership.

   i. New churches are planted by younger leaders to reach their generation.

      i. They raise up leaders from their generation and then grow older together.

      ii. Today's emerging generation is highly mobile. Rarely do they return home for their first career, marriage, and family.

      iii. We long ago lost the mentoring dynamic of Moses and Joshua, Barnabas and Saul, Paul and Timothy, Naomi and Ruth.

      iv. There's great spirituality among this generation.

      v. They are moving beyond secularism.

      vi. But they are exploring multiple spiritual options.

      vii. "I love Jesus, but I hate the church."

      viii. "I want to see it, not just hear about it."

      ix. The search for community

      x. Give up the glitz, give me authenticity.

3. The Proliferation of Bible Translations

   a. We've seen major shifts in worship styles and attendance patterns.

   b. Currently, worship attendance is in free fall. Likely under 10% in the city. May be slightly higher in certain suburbs.

   c. Before 1950, KJV used almost exclusively in churches with the American Standard Version (1901) used as a study Bible. I did most of my Bible memorization in the KJV.

   d. RSV NT: 1946, OT: 1952—in Evangelical circles this was viewed as the liberals' Bible.

   e. NASB NT: 1960, OT: 1971

   f. But the RSV and NASB continued to use old English. This led to a movement of new Bibles in the language of the common man.

   g. Dynamic Equivalence Translations and Paraphrases:

      i. Good News for Modern Man: NT 1966 (American Bible Society; Eugene Nida—lead of the translation department); OT 1976

      ii. Living Bible (Ken Taylor): 1971

      iii. The Message (Eugene Peterson): NT 1993, OT 2002

    h. NIV: NT 1973, OT 1978

    i. ESV: 2001

    j. The world Bible translation movement with the establishment of Wycliffe Bible Translators in 1942 (W. Cameron Townsend) and New Tribe Missions also in 1942 (Paul Fleming).

4. The Charismatic and Body Life Movements

    a. With the new translations came a seismic shift in understanding Ephesians 4:11–12:

        i. KJV: "For the perfecting of the saints, for the work of the ministry, for the edifying of the body of Christ."

        ii. NASB: "For the equipping of the saints for the work of service, to the building up of the body of Christ."

    b. Not just tongues and prophecy; much more about spiritual gifts and every members involvement in ministry.

    c. Clergy centered ministry to every member ministry

    d. Ray Stedman's Body Life, published in 1972—one body, many parts, members together

    e. Preaching as the sole paradigm of ministry to the multi-staff, diverse gifts model

    f. Decentralization of body life to home-based small groups

    g. The rise of the house church

    h. Multiple worship services, including Saturday evening

    i. A new understanding of spiritual gifts

    j. The disappearance of Blue Laws and Sunday as a quiet or sacred day

5. A new understanding of Mission

    a. Colonialization to indigenization to contextualization

    b. The epicenter of missions shifted in 1950 from Europe to the USA.

    c. That lasted only 24 years; by 1975, the sending of missionaries shifted from the USA to Latin America, Africa, and now Asia.

    d. The high cost of Western missions has increasingly made it difficult for the sending and supporting of career missionaries.

e. A move away from career missionaries to short-term missions (group mission trips) and connection of local church to local church vs. connection through mission agencies.

f. More recently, "foreign missions" has become "international missions," then "global missions," and now we speak of "glocal missions."

g. Immigrant churches are just as likely to plant churches back in their country of origin as they are to plant churches here.

6. **Shifts in leadership and theological training**

a. Most ministry decisions are made in response to changes that happened five or more years earlier.

b. Most leaders do not ask questions about how the environment will be changing in the next 5–10 years.

c. We need to retrain leadership to be proactive, not reactive, engagers of the community and cultural change occurring around them.

d. Seminary-trained leaders were taught grammatical-historical exegesis but were not taught to exegete culture and community. That needs to change.

e. The obsolescence of the M.Div. program

f. The majority of urban church leaders have not attended seminary. More have been trained in Bible institutes than in seminary.

g. The trend toward church-based apprenticeship models, especially in the independent, megachurch world, along the lines of Barnabas and Saul and Paul and Timothy.

h. There needs to be a rediscovery of godly character as the fundamental qualification for leadership.

i. We need to foster body interconnectedness to foster true life accountability and to provide the proper systems to sustain a lifetime in ministry service.

7. **Rediscovery of a holistic gospel:** the reuniting of word and deed ministry and the pursuit of justice expressed in mercy; this shift is coming from dynamics on the world scene which is now viewed in real time throughout the world—Southern Sudan and Darfur; Myanmar; West

Africa and tribal wars (colonization coming home to roost). The current debate on immigration, along with racial reconciliation, are crucial parts of the search for justice.

8. **A Final Challenge—Fractured Unity:** The decline of denominationalism and the search for new paradigms of interconnectedness

   a. Ephesians 4:3: "Make every effort to maintain the unity of the Spirit in the bond of peace."

   b. The hallmark of Philadelphia religion has been tolerance.

   c. Consequently, it's not an accident that denominationalism was birthed in Philadelphia.

   d. Philadelphia has been the epicenter of the great divides in the American Church.

      i. The Racial Divide of 1792—Richard Allen and the establishment of the African Methodist Episcopal Church (AME).

      ii. The liberal-fundamentalist split of the 1920s and 1930s and the negative influence of Carl McIntire deeply fractured evangelical Protestantism in Philadelphia.

   e. The little-spoken-of reality of independent evangelicalism coming out of Philadelphia

   f. The need for a generous ecclesiology: one body, many parts, members together

   g. Denominations are biblical only so far as they foster interconnectedness and missional partnership.

   h. They are unbiblical insofar as they limit and isolate churches from missional partnerships and interconnectedness.

   i. New paradigms of interconnectedness are emerging:

      i. This is an encouraging trend.

      ii. Community focused alliances: e.g., The Northwest Christian Alliance, South Philadelphia Alliance

      iii. Missional affinities: e.g., Acts 29 churches crossing denominational lines; Partners in Harvest and Koinonia Fellowship of Churches.